Barking	8724 8725	Thames View	8270 4164
Fanshawe	8270 4244	Valence	8270 6864
Marks Gate	8270 4165	Wantz	8270 4169
Markyate	8270 4137	Robert Jeyes	8270 4305
Rectory	8270 6233	Castle Green	8270 4166
Rush Green	8270 4304		

SHOPS

AUCTION HOUSES

AND MARKETS

MICHAEL LEECH

First published in 2006 by
New Holland Publishers (UK) Ltd
London • Cape Town • Sydney • Auckland

www.newhollandpublishers.com

Garfield House, 86–88 Edgware Road, London, W2 2EA,
United Kingdom

80 McKenzie Street, Cape Town 8001, South Africa

14 Aquatic Drive, Frenchs Forest, NSW 2086, Australia

218 Lake Road, Northcote, Auckland, New Zealand

10 9 8 7 6 5 4 3 2 1

ISBN 1 84537 256 5

Publishing Manager: Jo Hemmings
Senior Editors: Charlotte Judet and Steffanie Brown
Design: Alan Marshall
Maps: William Smuts
Production: Joan Woodroffe

Reproduction by Pica Digital Pte Ltd, Singapore
Printed and bound in Singapore by Kyodo Printing Co (Pte) Ltd

London Borough of
Barking & Dagenham

001	233	456
Askews		
708.051		£12.99

RnS

COVER AND PRELIMINARY PAGES
Front cover: A selection of early European sculptures and Old Masters drawings at
Joanna Booth.
Front flap: Oriental porcelain and ceramic vessels on show at Kevin Page Oriental Art.
Back cover: *left:* A coveted item is purchased at Bermondsey Market; *middle:* Fine
jewellery for sale at Grays Market; *right:* An auction in session at Lots Road Auctions.
Spine: The face of a longcase clock at Rafferty & Walwyn.
Opposite: Antiquarian books and ceramic vessels at Appley Hoare.

AUTHOR'S ACKNOWLEDGEMENTS
The author, Michael Leech, would like to thank all of the helpful friends who
made suggestions for outlets to include in the book. He would also like to thank
all of the courteous and patient antique dealers for their help.

CONTENTS

INTRODUCTION

If you are interested in antiques as a collector, a dealer, or just as a casual buyer, London is one of the top cities to visit. There are antiques aplenty here from all over the world, housed in venues where you can buy that elusive item you've long been hunting for, sell treasures you no longer favour, or just browse as a visitor, delighting in the wonderous offerings.

An Ancient Trading Centre

It all began with the Romans. The first armies crossed the Channel from Gaul, landing at what is now Sandwich. Marching up to the Thames, they set up camp just north of what is now London Bridge, establishing Londinium, their new capital. In Londinium, business began in earnest, and London has remained a trading and creative centre ever since, renowned for many centuries for its collectors and rich collections.

The acquisition and collection of precious old objects has long been a pastime and hobby of London's citizens. Beautiful, as well as practical, objects must have been made in many workshops close to the Thames, ranging from furniture to fabrics, glass to gems, and books to bibelots. In days long ago (and, arguably, today as well), these items we now call 'antiques' were essentially luxury items, restricted to the ruling classes. In fact, several English kings and queens had a crucial influence on the course and development of the artistic and crafts-making community: their interest in beautiful things led to their sponsorship of artists and craftsmen. A few of the royals were even genuine collectors; Richard II, for instance, loved the luxurious apparel of the High Gothic (his small, gilded prie dieux, one of the oldest objects in the National Gallery, illustrates this well). Cardinal Wolsey, Henry VIII, Queen Elizabeth I, Charles I and George IV were also all avid collectors.

Beginning in the late 16th century, British aristocrats also became collectors of antiques and antiquities, largely by virtue of having participated in what was known as the Grand Tour. The Grand Tour was a practice whereby young aristocrats would visit such places as Paris, Florence and Rome, often accompanied by a teacher, as the culmination of their classical education. Not only did these privileged men learn, they also shopped, and their discoveries and purchases directed a flow of rare and intriguing objects back to England. The third duke of Beaufort, for example, brought from Rome the third-century work named the Badminton Sarcophagus, which he proudly installed in his home in Gloucestershire. As the owners of such treasures have died and passed on their collections, many have come up for sale, or are now on show in our great museums and galleries.

From clocks to cabinetry, London's antique shops offer a range of wares.

The Ascent of the Middle Class

Antiques have always been fairly costly, their prices depending on their period, provenance and rarity value. Fashion has always added an element of desirability too, another factor reflected in the price of the object. Indeed, even when they were new, the finest antiques would not have been cheap, for such pieces would have been objects of great sophistication. For example, the incredible cabinetry and finish of French 17th- and 18th-century furniture, made with the best of craftsmanship, was never available to the masses.

That all changed, however, and slowly, these future-antiques entered the purview of the middle class. Starting with simple Tudor pieces and progressing into the 17th and 18th centuries, furniture began to actually mirror the ascent of a powerful middle class. Taste developed as people bettered themselves, and soon furniture and household goods were indications of the status and style of the family. In Britain, the great prevalence of 16th- and 17th-century oak furniture, then walnut, then imported mahogany and later exotic veneers, shows how the new affluence of a growing mercantile class, which first appeared during the Elizabethan period, led to the creation of many more superior goods.

In the early 19th century, after the rich styles of the Regency, came mass-production methods, and with these methods came a new surge of objects. This parade of good, solid, well-made pieces designed for use has resulted in an enormous antiques stock in England today.

7

Antiques and Their Collectors

An antique can be almost anything that is old and fascinating, and that means a huge range of articles. Many conventional antiques, such as porcelain, glass and pottery, have their admirers, but there are lots of unusual and sometimes odd things that are loved by particular collectors. Furthermore, antiques lovers come in all ages, and with a wide variety of likes and tastes: they are often a very knowledgeable and sophisticated audience. There are also a great many eager newcomers to antiques-buying and collecting; these prospective antiques owners are often young, and wish to discover for themselves the pleasure of owning beautiful and fascinating old things, from perfect pieces of Georgian furniture to fine pictures.

Given the vast range of antiques – and collectors – out there, this book attempts to cover a broad spread of antiquities, from the smartest of period furnishings on view in Mayfair and along Kensington Church Street, to shops selling retro clothing in Camden Town. Oddities are included in the book, too, with all sorts of possibilities in London outlets, not to mention the treasures that may be lurking in charity shops or in London's famous markets. I have also made reference to items as possible 'antiques of the future': present-day pieces that may grow gracefully into 'antiques status' in a few decades.

How to Buy Antiques

So how do you go about buying antiques? A good idea is to simply ask yourself what you like, and what you feel you might want to collect. Take, for example, an antique glass. Sets of glasses can be useful as well as decorative; single examples can look good in a display. Before you embark on your shopping expedition, you might want to read about the subject in order to learn simple basics, such as how to recognize blown, moulded or pressed glass. You may also decide to collect glasses from a specific geographical region or time period. Somewhere, something will spark your interest, and from then on you will search every shop and boot fair you pass!

On your travels, you will inevitably find certain shop and stall owners whom you like and trust, and you will no doubt go back to these dealers, having established a relationship with them. As you get to know a dealer, he or she will usually be fair with you and quote you good prices, because he or she will value your patronage and sense your increasing knowledge.

As with any item you buy, you should always be given an invoice for your antique purchases, with a description of the items you have bought, whether at a fair or at a shop or gallery: this will be essential if there is a problem later. For those who require an actual seal of authenticity, look for a golden chandelier symbol in the shop's window or at a fair; this signifies that the dealer is a member of LAPDA (The Association of Art and Antique Dealers). The BADA (British Antique Dealers'

Association) emblem, a blue and gold shield, offers the same authenticity guarantee. The latter association even offers to arbitrate, at no cost to the consumer, should a dispute arise between a consumer and a member dealer.

Good Hunting Grounds

As well as the antique shop per se, there are plenty of other establishments that are excellent sources of all sorts of antiquities and memorabilia. Antique markets, which tend to house numerous dealers within a single site, are always a good bet. Auction houses, which tend to be more up-market, are likewise a good resource for those who can afford them. London is also home to many shopping arcades, located mostly off Piccadilly and Regent streets, as well as in the suburbs. At the other end of the price spectrum are the humble junk and charity shops, which should never be underestimated as possible sources for great and worthy treasures.

Antique Markets

Markets have always existed in London, as in all major cities, as the supply of food and goods to the populace has always been an urgent necessity. The site of the original Roman mart, a set of stalls selling goods and fresh produce – and undoubtedly the main source for daily purchases 2,000 years ago – still lies beneath the present-day City of London. One such market, situated off Gracechurch Street, in The City, still remains: the ornate Victorian pillared and porticoed Leadenhall Market, which dates back to the 14th century.

For a long time – indeed right up to the middle of the 20th century – markets were still the place to buy almost everything the corner shop lacked, from food and drink to household articles and furniture. (My grandfather purchased two longcase clocks at the local cattle market in Norfolk in 1900: they cost £1 each!) However, it is doubtful that markets were ever as diverse and different as they are now, for in today's London markets you can buy almost anything, from flowers to cosmetics.

Antique markets are, however, a relatively recent arrival. London has several major

A trawl through a market stall can result in first-rate treasures.

A good auctioneer will generate excitement about the item.

ones, all noted here, and some of these – such as Bermondsey in the East, and Portobello Road in the West – are almost household names. These markets are always fascinating places for discovering unique and special items, whatever their purpose, and are often great fun to meander around, searching for treasures with a history.

It is often thought a good idea to bargain at a market. In truth, the benefit of this action depends on the seller: most stall owners will have priced their goods carefully, padding the price in order to protect against bargainers. Be warned as well that many dealers expect bargaining, but may not be very polite about it. So try if you wish, but remember that it is not part of a game, as it is in some countries.

Auction Houses

There are several internationally known auction houses in London, most of them renowned for frequent sales of top price articles, such as Old Master paintings. How often one reads of a rare Renaissance work, or an Impressionist canvas, up for sale and often fetching millions. Some are bought for museums, some for private collections, and some end up in bank vaults as collateral for businesses. London's auction houses, most with additional addresses abroad in New York and other major centres, ring up the news headlines at such times, yet most auction sales go on every day pretty much unnoticed except by collectors and dealers.

Auction houses can offer general antiques, but they also often have special sales of associated items such as specific periods of furniture, pottery, porcelains, silver, pictures, mirrors or even stamps. The specialist collector will always be drawn to these events, as will be sellers, knowing that their special items may well attract furious bidding. Recently, a friend waited for a specific sales event and sold a 17th-century mirror (with original glass and unrestored – all 'pluses') at auction, and netted perhaps three times what she might have made at a non-specific sale.

Auctions are well advertised ahead of time (you can be put on mailing lists), and can take a whole day. They are usually free, but sometimes there is a ticketed entrance. There will be preview times when you can see the goods on offer – very necessary, as you will often be buying 'as found', so check carefully. If the event is a popular one, the day of sale may be crowded, so arrive in good time to get a seat. There may be a price indication, or there may not be. If you plan to bid, register your name with one of the auctioneer's assistants. At London events you will be issued with a number to hold up; in the country, a wave usually suffices. If you are successful, an assistant will come and take your details.

When bidding at an auction, bid clearly as the sum asked for is announced. Sometimes, the auctioneer's price will have been optimistic, so the asking price will drop. When in competition with other bidders, an affirmative or negative nod is also recognized. It's all a kind of game (though serious money is often involved), and can be quite exciting if you are up for a contest to acquire a desirable object.

Remember that you will pay a premium on top of your bid price, as will the seller. You can enquire about the amount before you sit down. It is sometimes as low as 10 per cent, but it can be more. Finally, to help you cart away your winnings, there are usually porters on hand to assist you with large or cumbersome articles.

Shopping Arcades

Shopping arcades lined with a variety of pocket-sized shops are a feature in London. Most are located in the centre of the city, with others in the West End; still others are in the suburbs. The notable examples in Central London are the Burlington, Piccadilly, and Princes arcades. In the City, the Royal Exchange mart, founded in Tudor times, was a sort of early arcade.

Despite being a quintessential London shopping venue, shopping arcades did not originate here. They began in Bologna and spread into other Italian cities, resulting in such spectacular spaces as the great Gallerias in Milan and Naples. By the early 19th century, they were common in most European cities, and went on to become increasingly popular. In the United Kingdom there were obvious reasons for their popularity: the lined-up shops are huddled closely together under one roof, creating an agreeable promenade that is covered overhead, to guard against London's notoriously bad weather. Some London arcades contain antique shops, although being necessarily small premises these tend to stock tiny objects.

Charity Shops

Don't ignore the humble charity shop in London. There are quite a few of them, in all areas, often right on main shopping streets; ubiquitous examples are Help The Aged, Oxfam, Sue Ryder and Dr Barnardo's. The idea behind these shops is that people will bring in and donate all sorts of articles, from jumble to gems, some not needed by their owners, some generous gifts of valuables, for sale to anyone to benefit a range of charities. They are then checked and put out for sale. A purchase made in these shops thus means a donation to a worthy cause, so request receipts for possible tax deduction purposes.

Although much of their stock is predictable – clothes, furs, leather goods, books, records, boots and shoes, conventional china and glass, pottery, metalware, small decorative items, plastic toys and board games – treasures can indeed still be found amongst the trivia. As these venues are popular for bargain-hunters, stock often moves fast. Many of these small shops are located in smart areas, so gifts from wealthy residents or house and flat clearances can bring quite surprising items, and many an antique has got back on the market this way. If you get to know the manager and his or her volunteers, they will often look out for any particular thing you may be looking for.

Salvage Yards

At these venues, items for sale often have an architectural aspect, such as pieces discarded from demolished houses and commercial buildings. These can include ironwork, statues and doors, old beams, floorboards, skirtings, friezes and roof tiles, classical pillars, wood- or stone-framed windows, terracotta decorations, grandiose marble-framed fireplaces complete with grates, even whole conservatories and period staircases. Often there will be outdoor ornaments, and antique brick and stone garden features, too. All get a recycling into newly built houses wanting an 'old' look, or are added to newly adapted flats, particularly those being carved out of once-commercial buildings. Other salvaged items become part of new 'theme' restaurants, or are used to decorate hotel foyers. Salvage yards are essentially the 'house and garden' equivalent of a junk shop, as their wares are much more bulky and heavy.

If shopping at a salvage yard, remember that you will need transport and help to get your items home. While some places will deliver, it is wise to learn about the shop's delivery and installation policy before you go out on your search.

Salvage yards sell all manner of architectural antiques, from small fittings to period staircases.

How to Use this Book

Written for both visitors and locals, this book aims to act as a guide to antique shops, markets and auction houses throughout Greater London and a short distance beyond (accessible in a day trip). From the priciest shops of Kensington to the eclectic, bargain-friendly venues on the Lillie Road, and from the traditional to the eccentric, this book will tell you where to go to buy exactly what you're looking for.

As an adjunct to the listed shops, markets and auction houses, we have also suggested some venues that you might like to visit while you're in the area. These are largely places that have collections or period interiors likely to further the knowledge and awareness of antique collectors.

Towards the end of the book is a list of some of the prestigious antique fairs held in London throughout the year. This list is by no means exhaustive; there are many smaller, lesser-known fairs held each year within London and throughout the country. For a detailed calendar of antique-related events, check www.artefact.co.uk.

The book's final pages cover such important information as shipping, valuation and insurance. Some good advice on taking care in London, staying within the export laws and protecting oneself from fraudulent vendors is also provided. There is also a short section on hunting for buried treasure for the more adventurous readers!

The Entries

At the top of each entry you will find the full name of the shop, the address, telephone number, website or e-mail address, and details on public transport and opening hours. Below this information is an at-a-glance brief indicating whether the entry is a shop, auction house or market, and the types of wares it sells. The main entry paragraph indicates in detail the types of wares sold at the venue, along with any services offered.

The Photographs

The photographs show a selection of shops, markets and auction houses that are particularly photogenic and illustrate the diversity of outlets throughout London. The photographs are not meant as an indicator of hierarchy.

The Maps

At the start of each chapter covering a section of London, a map gives a geographical reference to the areas covered. Each of the shops, auction houses and markets within the chapter are plotted on the map. Different icons represent each type of venue:

shop 👆 auction house ✎ market 🏪

MARYLEBONE

FITZROVIA

BLOOMSBURY

ST PANCRAS

SOHO

MAYFAIR

ST JAMES'S

Hyde Park

Green Park

BROMPTON

BELGRAVIA

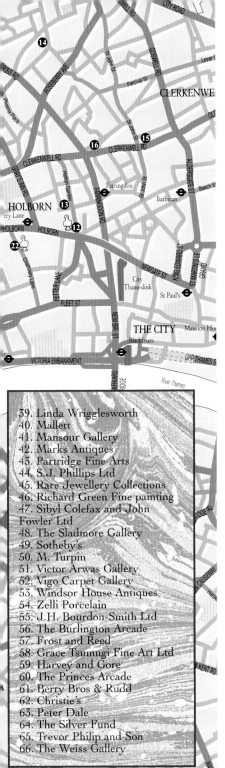

Central London

The heart of London is characterized by its greatly contrasting establishments. There are smart galleries and specialist shops of all kinds in Mayfair, a range of bookshops along the Charing Cross Road, while in literary Bloomsbury rare books rub shoulders with shops selling genuine antiquities. Piccadilly Circus is home to perhaps the most famous shopping arcades in London, filled with antique offerings, among others. There are few antique shops in Covent Garden now, but the market itself can still be depended upon to throw up some treasures. And then there is The City, with its tiny lanes and famous historic buildings.

Belgravia

This has been a very smart – and expensive – location in which to live for almost 200 years. South of Hyde Park and west of Buckingham Palace, it was developed from a marsh in the early 19th century by the Grosvenor family. Then an insalubrious place, once drained and cleaned it became fashionable and elegant with its spacious squares and bold stucco-fronted terraces of large houses and villas, mostly cream-painted. Many embassies and consulates are located here, partly due to its proximity to the palaces and government offices. There are also some very chic shops here, mostly in small malls adjoining streets with modern, covered arcades.

Norman Adams Ltd

8–10 Hans Road, SW3 * 020 7589 5266 * www.normanadams.com * Tube: Knightsbridge; Bus: 19, 22, 137, C1 * Mon–Fri 09:00 – 17:30; Sat and Sun by appointment

Large store: 18th-century English furniture, clocks, needlework

A spacious and well-stocked store just off the main Brompton road. Behind an original Edwardian façade, the showrooms with their high ceilings contain a large stock of fine 18th-century English furniture. Quality is emphasized, with condition, colour and patina of prime importance as the hallmarks of the business. There are also chandeliers, clocks and barometers, needlework and objets d'art. *The Norman Adams Collection*, a book of 18th-century English furniture, makes a good introduction to the subject and period (£45 on sale here, or by post overseas).

Andre De Cacqueray

227 Ebury Street, SW1 * 020 7730 5000 * Tube: Sloane Square; Bus: 11, 211, 239 * Mon–Sat 10:00 – 18:00

Antique shop: 18th- and 19th-century French furniture items

This shop deals primarily in 18th- and 19th-century French furniture, with some Continental examples sold as well. There is also an interior design service.

Fine 18th-century English antiques are for sale at Norman Adams.

Harrod's Old Maps and Prints

87-135 Brompton Road, SW1 * **020 7730 1234** *
www.harrods.com * **Tube: Knightsbridge; Bus: 14, 74, 414, C1**
* **Mon—Sat 10:00—20:00, Sun 12:00—18:00**

Department store: prints, engravings, maps, English and French 19th-century furniture

This well-known Knightsbridge department store, with its palatial terra cotta façade, cannot be missed, especially when illuminated at night. The antique maps section on the third floor is devoted to framed prints, engravings and watercolours, as well as to maps dating from the 16th century up to 1900. They also sell a variety of English and French late 19th-century furniture.

Jeremy Ltd

29 Lowndes Street, SW1 * **020 7823 2923** *
www.jeremy.ltd.uk * **Tube: Knightsbridge; Bus: 19, 22, 137, C1**
* **Mon—Fri 08:30—18:00; Sat by appointment**

Gallery: 18th- and 19th-century furniture, glass chandeliers

A smart and spacious gallery, this venue offers a range of 18th- and 19th-century furniture, bibelots and objets d'art. Handsome period glass chandeliers are on show, too. Most items are English, with some French and Russian offerings as well.

Joss Graham Oriental Textiles

10 Eccleston Street, SW1 * **020 7730 4370** * **e-mail:**
joss.graham@btinternet.com * **Tube: Victoria; Bus: 11, 211,**
239, C1, C10 * **Mon—Fri 10:00—18:00, or by appointment**

Two-level store: Oriental textiles, fabrics, primitive art

Established for 25 years, this store boasts two levels stuffed with exotic textiles from all over the world. African, Asian, Indian and Middle Eastern fabrics tumble before the eye in a profusion of shawls, saris, embroideries and even exotic tribal costumes. Primitive art is also on display, including masks and sculptures. Kilims and rugs are sold here, too.

Bloomsbury

Made famous by its many literary associations (take a stroll and note the blue plaques), this primarily residential quarter of central London has some good shops, especially for old and new books and prints. Ancient artifacts, from figurines to clay lamps, can also be found here. Occasionally, additional antiquities appear, such as reading and storage racks, print screens and incunabula. The quality of the items offered at these specialist shops is often exceptional.

Bloomsbury Auctions

Bloomsbury House, 24 Maddox Street, W1 * **020 7495 9494** * www.bloomsburyauctions.com * Tube: Oxford Circus; Bus: 3, 6, 12, 13, 88, 94 * Mon–Fri 09:30–5:30

Auction house: books, manuscripts, maps

Twenty-four sales a year are held here. Items for sale include second-hand and vintage books, medieval manuscripts, autograph letters, prints, paintings, maps, historic documents, drawings, photographs and posters. Single items as well as entire collections are bought and sold. Valuations done.

Imago Mundi Antique Maps Ltd

40a Museum Street, WC1 * **020 7405 7477** * Tube: Tottenham Court Road; Bus: 25, 242 * Mon–Fri 09:30–5:30

Antique shop: antique maps and views from the 15th to the 19th centuries

Based in the heart of London, near the British Museum, the maps sold here include renderings of the world, Africa, the Americas, Asia, the Pacific and Australasia, and Europe, as well as astronomical maps and celestial charts.

Jarndyce Antiquarian Booksellers

46 Great Russell Street, WC1 * 020 7631 4220 * Tube:
Tottenham Court Road; Bus: 25, 242 * Mon–Fri 10.30 – 17.30

*Antique shop: books published before 1920; books and pamphlets of the
17th and 18th centuries; 19th-century fiction*

Jarndyce Antiquarian Booksellers have been selling books published before 1920 for
34 years. The building itself has been a bookshop for over a century, and retains
many period features. The ground floor has recently been renovated to recreate a
19th-century bookshop within an 18th-century building, incorporating panelling, a
working fireplace and original wooden floors. Major catalogues are devoted to a
series of subjects, including Charles Dickens, the Romantics, books and pamphlets
of the 17th and 18th centuries, female authors, plays and the theatre, London books
and maps and 19th-century fiction.

Michael Finney Antique Prints

31 Museum Street, WC1 * 020 7631 3533 *
www.michaelfinney.co.uk * Tube: Tottenham Court Rd;
Bus: 7, 10, 24, 29, 73 * Mon–Sat 10:00 – 18:00

Gallery: antique maps, prints, portraits

Whether you are a serious collector or you just want a fine antique map for your
study, this is an ideal gallery to explore. Situated opposite the British Museum, here
you'll find decorative framed and unframed prints from many artists, including such
famous names as Piranesi, David Roberts and William Hogarth. There is a range of
caricatures and portraits, with topographical and architectural subjects as well.
Michael Finney and his staff are on hand with helpful advice.

Pollock's Theatre Shop

1 Scala Street, WI * 020 7636 3452 * Tube: Goode Street;
Bus: 10, 24, 29, 73 * Mon–Sat 10:00 – 17:00

Antique shop: children's toys (model theatres), books, games, memorabilia

On the corner of Scala and Whitfield Streets, this is a delightful shop containing a
marvellous jumble of children's toys, books, games and memorabilia. Founded in

Jarndyce is one of the oldest and most respected bookshops in London.

Hoxton, East London, it recalls the Victorian shop interiors one used to find throughout London. Packed with oddities, it winds through small rooms on two levels. The main interest is model theatres – reproductions of old theatres that work. The renowned 'make-it-yourself' cardboard playhouses, with cut-out costumed performers, are also for sale, along with scripts from serious plays to pantomimes.

While you're in the area...
THE CHARLES DICKENS MUSEUM

48 Doughty Street, WC1 * 020 7405 2127 * www.dickensmuseum.com * Tube: Russell Square, Chancery Lane; Bus: 7, 17, 19, 38, 45, 46 * Mon–Sat 10:00–17:00, Sun 11:00–17:00 * Admission fee

Dickens was always a Londoner. As a little boy, he toiled in a wretched riverside warehouse, where Charing Cross now stands, pasting labels on pots of blacking. From this miserable existence he made his way to a smart terraced house in Bloomsbury, and became a highly favoured novelist. He lived in several houses in central London, all of which are marked with blue plaques. This house makes a most evocative museum. Victorian memorabilia and furniture abounds, from bedrooms to basement. Indeed, the domestic interior of the house is a veritable heaven for lovers of everything 19th century.

POLLOCK'S TOY MUSEUM

1 Scala Street, WC1 * 020 7636 3452 * www.pollockstoymuseum.com * Tube: Goodge Street; Bus: 24, 134, 390 * Mon–Sat 10:00–17:00 * Admission fee

Located in two 18th-century houses, this museum has an assortment of historic toys from all over the world. Most exhibits date from the last 200 years, but there are also some older pieces, including an Egyptian clay mouse dating from 2000 BC. The museum's small rooms are crammed with toys, including dolls, puppets, teddy bears, cars, trains and construction sets. There is also a toyshop offering traditional toys and model theatres (see page 20).

Charing Cross

Charing Cross is the centre of London for all measures of distance, encompassing the grand Trafalgar Square, from which several major thoroughfares open out, from Whitehall to the Mall running to Buckingham Palace. This is the place in London to buy books, both new and old. The new bookshops lie mostly between Leicester Square and Tottenham Court Road stations. At the Trafalgar Square end of the road, both the National Gallery and the National Portrait Gallery sell a plethora of art books. Off the lower part of the road, between Leicester Square and Charing Cross stations, is Cecil Court, with its specialist antiquarian bookshops – and higher prices.

Cecil Court

Alley connecting Charing Cross Road and St Martin's Lane *
www.cecilcourt.co.uk * **Tube: Leicester Square; Bus: 24, 176**
A treasure spot, this old-fashioned parade of fascinating shops is exactly the sort of enclave that once existed in many London districts, for the shop fronts have not been altered in more than a century. Here you will find a number of little shops offering a good selection of wares, particularly prints, posters, stamps, bank notes and rare and antiquarian books, with many shops displaying their goods on outside shelves. Below is a list of some of the shops at Cecil Court.

DAVID DRUMMOND
11 Cecil Court, WC2 * **020 7836 1142** * **e-mail:**
drummond@popt.fsnet.co.uk * **Mon–Fri 11:00 – 14:30,**
15:30 – 17:45

For the lover of drama and music halls, this is a veritable treasure house. Masses of theatrical memorabilia are piled on shelves, and the walls are lined with all sorts of intriguing articles, from puppets to playbills, all in one glorious clutter. There are many original music hall and Victorian posters, along with other visual material, and theatre photographs and programmes bulge out of boxes. The affable Mr Drummond will search out that which you request in his overflowing treasure trove of material.

INDOSTAN
14 Cecil Court, WC2 * 020 7836 2234 * www.indostan.co.uk * Mon–Sat 11:00 – 19:00

A sheaf of beautifully detailed and painted shadow puppets, from the isles of Indonesia and Java to Afghanistan, makes a lively stage of this crowded shop's window, the exotic stock tumbling to the pavement outside during the day. This is a shop which doesn't have to announce what it deals in – its goods are obviously Middle and Far Eastern. Here you will find rugs, hangings, old artifacts, and a vast array of shadow puppets, which are the special feature. The owners present readings, concerts and performances too, so you may see how the puppets appear when they are 'at work', turning the shop into a living theatre.

MARK SULLIVAN ANTIQUES AND DECORATIVES
9 Cecil Court, WC2 * 020 7836 7056 * Mon–Sat 10:00 – 19:00

An eclectic mix of intriguing old objects all very neatly arranged in the window and on the loaded shelves inside. Behind the green-painted façade there is a vast mass of goods to explore here, with a host of small, interesting items. You will find vases and lamps, bibelots and busts, statues and scent bottles, tea pots and tankards, patch and snuff boxes (in metal and porcelain), antique toys (including the ever-intriguing moving mechanical ones), and even some old brass bathroom fittings. There are also Art Nouveau figurines, along with many Art Déco items.

NIGEL WILLIAMS
25 Cecil Court, WC2 * 020 7836 7757 * www.nigelwilliams.com * Mon–Sat 10:00 – 18:00

For collectors of first editions, this small, elegant bookshop, with its chaste white ceiling and walls, old wooden floors and modern lighting, is a 'must visit' address. 'Fine and rare books, literary first editions, detective fiction, children's and illustrated books' are announced by the knowledgeable owner, who offers unobtrusive, polite help. The accent is firmly on modern first editions, but there is also a range of unusual books here. The price range is vast too – from £10 to £50,000. The fascinating children's and 19th-century stock is to be found on the lower basement level. Some pictures and prints are also displayed.

PETER ELLIS BOOKSELLER
18 Cecil Court, WC2 * **020 7836 8880** * **www.peter-ellis.co.uk** * **Mon–Fri 10:30 – 19:00, Sat 10:30 – 17:30**

A loaded nest of shelves by the door and a rack of books are placed outside this dealer's neat and inviting shop. Here, browsing, which used to be such a London pleasure, is very much encouraged. Inside, atop grey wooden floors, a series of shelves support a large, well arranged stock. The special angle here is modern literature, poetry, illustrated books and history, mostly first editions. The owner is at hand to help his customers.

RED SNAPPER BOOKS
22 Cecil Court, WC2 * **020 7240 2075** *
www.redsnapperbooks.com * **Mon–Sat 10:00 – 18:00**

A telling sign is the sculpture of the fish in fierce red that hangs above the window display here. Within, it's a haven for an odd subject and an eccentric generation – the

Indostan sells an impressive range of working shadow puppets from Asia.

beatnik and counter culture of mid-20th century. All of the many pictures and arti-facts here tie in to that time, with some telling photographs and cartoons in lurid colours. There is a selection of unusual framed prints too. Even the floor is odd, cov-ered in a sort of pimpled zinc sheeting that climbs up the walls, and yet is somehow appropriate, for this is very much a one-off place.

REES & O'NEILL
7 Cecil Court, WC2 * 020 7836 3336 * www.rees-oneill.com
* Mon–Fri 10:00 – 18:00, Sat 10:00 – 17:00

A charming shop for the dedicated collector, who should feel at home here with old wooden floors and lots of books lining both the inside and outside of the narrow premises. For bargains, out front on a rack is a range of books, all priced at a pound. Within the shop, the volumes are mostly modern first editions – their special inter-est – along with rare books on art, design and illustration. A mixed array of prints and some interesting portraits hang on the walls. The staff is welcoming here, and are willing to help with any enquiries.

STOREY'S LTD
3 Cecil Court, WC2 * 020 7836 3777 * e-mail:
storeysltd@btinternet.com * Mon–Tues, Thurs–Fri 10:00 –
19:00, Wed & Sat 10:00 – 18:00

Engravings and prints in profusion are displayed here in well spaced ranks on the white walls, and with good lighting they are easy to inspect. Quality, order and personal knowledge are evident at this antiquarian bookseller. Fine quality hand-coloured works always in stock include naval, military and sporting subjects, as well as natural history. Old maps and views are also for sale, along with large theatre prints. A speciality are lithographs of Egypt, Nubia and the Holy Land. Fine bind-ings are also a special interest, and if required, there is also a framing service. Old magazines feature here, too, on display outside the shop.

TIM BRYARS LTD
8 Cecil Court, WC2 * 020 7836 1901 * www.timbryars.co.uk
* Mon–Fri 11:00 – 18:00, Sat 12:00 – 17:00

An elegant place, calm and well ordered, with a range of prints neatly placed on its plain walls. There is a splendid array of old maps, mostly 16th to 18th century, and most from European sources — you can get a 17th-century work for £600, or go all the way up to as much as £6,000 for a rarity. On the second level you will find shelves of early printed books, the topics ranging from the classics to travel.

TRAVIS & EMERY
17 Cecil Court, WC2 * 020 7240 2129 * www.travis-and-emery.com * Mon–Sat 10:15 – 18:45, Sun 12:00 – 18:00

If music is an interest for you, make a visit to this cluttered, atmospheric shop dealing in antiquarian music and literature. A large print chest squats on the red linoleum serving as a table. Under an appropriately Victorian pressed ceiling, an array of vocal, choral, instrumental and miniature scores of operas, operettas, musicals and choruses is on hand, suspended like festoons on lines. Many of the scores have charming period illustrations in colour, making them an attractive item for framing, as well as being of practical use for music lovers. Photographs and libretti are also stored on both the racks and on the white walls. Both old and new books on all aspects of music are available.

WATKINS BOOKS
19 & 21 Cecil Court, WC2 * 020 7836 2182 * www.watkinsbooks.com * Mon–Sat 11:00–19:00

There are two Watkins shops on the Court, for those seeking books on unusual cults, beliefs and old religions. Both are atmospheric, as well as aromatic, owing to the scent of incense. Here there is an accent on the exotic, even occult, and 'Mind, Body and Spirit' books are sold as well. There is also a lecture room on the premises. The original shop at number 19 is wide-windowed, with a green- and gold-painted façade; this shop offers tarot card readings. The shop at number 21 is equally charged with the exotic, with even its carpet adorned with Egyptian motifs.

THE WITCH BALL
2 Cecil Court, WC2 * 020 7836 2922 * www.thewitchball.com * Mon–Sat 10:30 – 18:30

This well-lit shop has a special, very visual appeal, for it stocks and displays large theatrical posters. Many of these are French, and are therefore witty and gaily designed for the pleasure of a knowing Parisian public. The posters are not all large however; smaller ones are also available, and all tend to be lively, highly coloured and demanding of attention — which was, of course, their original purpose. They make an arresting spectacle, mostly ready-framed, and ideal for displaying on large, bare walls such as those currently being exposed in warehouse conversions. Antique prints are sold here as well.

Old French prints and posters are plentiful at The Witch Ball.

The City and Clerkenwell

The City stretches back to Roman occupation 2,000 years ago; the centre of the Roman settlement was just north of London Bridge. Today, 'The City' is one of London's primary business districts, and is filled mostly with huge office blocks. Some old streets still exist, but the ancient buildings and terraced houses are now gone. The few remaining old structures include various monuments, guild halls and churches. Just north of The City, a minute from the roaring Farringdon Road, lies Clerkenwell, an old village drawn long ago into the urban sprawl of the expanding city. The area is now a haven for art galleries and artists.

Andrew R. Ullman Ltd

10 Hatton Garden, EC1 * 020 7405 1877 * www.arullman.com * Tube: Chancery Lane; Bus: 25, 242, 341 * Mon–Sat 09:00 – 17:00

Antique shop: specializing in antique and second-hand gold, silver and gem jewellery; Victorian and Georgian periods a speciality

A family-run antique business with a large selection of jewellery, watches, silverware and objets d'art. Repairs, restoration and valuations undertaken. Online catalogue.

Berganza

88–90 Hatton Garden, EC1 * 020 7430 0393 * e-mail: info@berganza.com * Tube: Chancery Lane; Bus: 17, 45, 46, 55 * Mon–Sat 10:00 – 17:00

Family-owned antique shop: antique jewellery, repairs and valuations

Hatton Garden was once London's diamond district, and is still lined with modern jewellery shops. It used to have many family-owned businesses, though nowadays, shops like this one are a comparative rarity. 'There are hardly any of us dealing with antique jewellery now', the affable owner says. He offers Georgian pieces, but prefers to sell Art Déco and Art Nouveau designs. Repairs and valuations undertaken.

City Clocks

31 Amwell Street, EC1 * 020 7278 1154 or 0800 783 4587 *
www.cityclocks.co.uk * Tube: Angel; Bus: 30, 73, 205, 214 *
Mon–Fri 08:30 – 17:30, Sat 09:30 – 14:30, or by appointment

Antique shop: antique timepieces, 18th- and 19th-century furniture

This small and atmospheric shop, established for over 55 years, sells a vast array of antique timepieces, from wall to longcase, and from most time periods. These pieces are complemented by 18th- and 19th-century furniture, as well as some decorative items. A restoration service is offered for clocks and watches.

Frosts of Clerkenwell Ltd

60-62 Clerkenwell Road, EC1 * 020 7253 0315 *
www.frostsofclerkenwell.co.uk * Tube: Barbican; Bus: 55, 243
* Mon–Fri 09:30 – 16:30

Large shop: clocks, barometers, watches

This large shop is located at the northern end of Hatton Garden. The shop has been established for over 70 years, so the owners are well informed about their stock, which includes a wide range of clocks, barometers and associated items, as well as a selection of antique timepieces. A restoration service is offered for clocks and watches.

Lesley Craze Gallery

33-35a Clerkenwell Green, EC1 * 020 7608 0393 *
www.lesleycrazegallery.co.uk * Tube: Farringdon; Bus: 55, 63,
243 * Tues–Sat 10:00 – 17:30

Gallery: jewellery

Here in the centre of Clerkenwell Green is a new and welcome addition. This gallery is very modern, and is comprised of a smart black and white set of rooms. The jewellery here is definitely for collectors seeking 'antiques of the future': stylish, sculptural pieces, especially pendants and necklets from European, American and Australian artists, are for sale.

Covent Garden

This was once a nuns' home, hence 'convent garden'. In the 17th century it was the most fashionable place to live, and many grand people resided here. It is famed in literature for being part of the opening scene of George Bernard Shaw's *Pygmalion*, which became the musical *My Fair Lady*. The central piazza lost its flower and vegetable markets in the 1980s, and since then, many fashionable boutiques have flooded in, often replacing antique and book shops. Today, Covent Garden is one of London's most popular tourist destinations. The Jubilee Hall plays host every Monday to an important antique market.

Dress Circle

57–59 Monmouth Street, WC2 * 020 7240 2227 * www.dresscircle.com * Tube: Covent Garden; Bus: 24, 176 * Mon–Sat 10:00 – 18:30

Antique shop: theatre and show music 'collectables'

The accent here is on the theatre, with the Georgian shop front stuffed with material. This shop is especially good for show music, so if you are a fan, this is a clubby place for gossip and research: check the message boards. Although this shop sells mostly CDs, DVDs, videos and books, it also has old posters and sheet music – so it is collectables you may find here rather than old items, but there are personality recordings as well as nostalgia. There is a box for those wanting to unload theatre programmes and such, the proceeds from which are donated to Aids charities.

Treadwell's

34 Tavistock Street, WC2 * 020 7240 8906 * www.treadwells-london.com * Tube: Covent Garden; Bus: 139, 176, 623 * Mon–Sun 12:00 – 19:00

Antique shop: second-hand books on mysterious topics, magic and myth

Witch balls and heresy? Wizardry and tribal cults? This unusual bookshop, marked with fluttering draperies, has it all. Inside, chairs and benches make a welcoming, atmospheric place in which to linger, even if the antiques available are mostly second-hand volumes on mysterious topics. Volumes are crowded on the shelves, arranged in categories from culture and religion to astrology and tribal cults. Topics concern mysteries from the Dark to the Middle Ages, and range around the world through Africa, Asia and Russia, as well as Europe. Magic and myth link hands here, and the service is friendly and helpful. Old books are bought, too.

Vertigo Galleries

22 Wellington Street, WC2 * 020 7836 9252 * www.vertigogalleries.com * Tube: Covent Garden; Bus: 139, 176, 623 * Tues–Sat 11:00 – 18:00, Mon by appointment

Memorabilia shop: film memorabilia – posters, lobby cards

Just around the corner from Treadwell's is a new shop offering vintage and original film posters, lobby cards and other movie memorabilia. Examples are shown in the large window; inside they are presented in an almost minimalistic way. Mostly for sale are classic posters, which are the most popular items; these can be framed here, too. Although there's not much of a welcome upon entry, there are big armchairs that you can sink into as you scan through the rare items on offer.

Covent Garden Market

The Piazza, WC2 * 020 7836 9136 * www.coventmarket.com * Tube: Covent Garden; Bus: 139, 176, 623 * Antiques Market operates Mondays only, 05:00 – 12:00

Market: antiques and bric-à-brac

In an area where markets have been held since the 14th century, Covent Garden's Jubilee Market is unique in that it is the only market in the capital owned wholly by the traders. Three groups of traders are present at this famous market: those dealing in antiques, those dealing in arts and crafts, and those dealing in general goods. For those interested in antiques, the central Jubilee Hall plays host every Monday to an antique and bric-à-brac market. It is held on the ground floor, from the wee hours of the morning until mid-afternoon. Professional buyers from leading auction houses often make an early appearance.

Fitzrovia

Running to the north edge of Soho, Fitzrovia is comprised of a net of narrow streets spreading east of the main artery, Tottenham Court Road. Historically, the area was home to many writers and artists, notably George Bernard Shaw, who lived at 29 Fitzroy Square, and Virginia Woolf, who later occupied the same address. Largely a 19th-century layout, Fitzrovia was invented as a separate district in the 1930s, and today the area is home to many art galleries – note those along Charlotte Street, which is also famed for its restaurants and pubs. Despite recent gentrification – and corresponding high rental prices – Fitzrovia continues to attract Bohemian artist and writer residents.

The Samuel French bookshop

52 Fitzroy Street W1 * 020 7387 9373 * www.samuelfrench-london.co.uk * Tube: Warren Street; Bus: 24, 134, 390 * Mon–Fri 09:30–17:30, Sat 11:00–17:00

Bookshop: *theatre scripts and plays*

This is a renowned, established bookshop specializing in drama and royalty collection, and selling scripts to companies and individuals, both professional and amateur. If you are interested in theatre scripts and plays, this is the shop to visit – it's still a family business, which has been running for an impressive 175 years. Currently over 2,000 titles are in print, and in the atmospheric shop itself there's a large stock of books on many aspects of the theatre, from both British and American publishers, along with play scripts. The shop keeps a comprehensive backlist and a mailing list, and they update their website regularly.

Holborn

Standing at the crossing of Holborn and High Holborn, this area sits on the fringe of the West End, bordering The City on its eastern side. Although Holborn is very much a business area, it is also a lively part of London, with plenty of action in its cafés and pubs. Holborn has a fairly ordinary run of shops, but there is one very important exception: the famous London Silver Vaults, a virtual mecca of all things silver. Another fixture in the area is the world-renowned British Museum.

Lovers of antique silver should not miss the London Silver Vaults.

London Silver Vaults

53-64 Chancery Lane (off Fleet Street), WC2 * 020 7242 3844
* www.thesilvervaults.com * Tube: Chancery Lane; Bus: 23,
341 * Mon–Fri 09:00 – 17:30, Sat 09:00 – 13:00

Salesrooms: articles in precious metals

These famous salesrooms are the oldest of their kind in the world, found under-
ground at the vaults. The vaults consist of 40 cellar spaces, each measuring about 70
square feet, with plain brick walls. Allow a fair amount of time if you visit, because
there is lots to see. Renters of the crowded rooms are all specialists, their shelves
lined with all kinds of high quality precious objects, from presentation pieces to
domestic dishes and bowls. Almost everything is in silver and silver-gilt, but there is
some gold. Expensive in general, but well worth an extended visit if articles in
precious metals appeal to you.

While you're in the area...
THE BRITISH MUSEUM

Great Russell Street, WC1 * 020 7323 8299 *
www.thebritishmuseum.ac.uk * Tube: Holborn; Bus: 7, 8,
19, 25, 38, 55 * Sat–Wed 10:00 – 17:30, Thurs–Fri
10:00 – 20:30 * Free admission

This world-famous museum admits 6.5 million visitors a year, and it's no wonder, as there is so much to see here. As well as the famed Greek, Egyptian and
Assyrian gallery sections, there are whole rooms devoted to important antiquities and antique articles, from Roman jewels and 17th-century lace to longcase
clocks and armorial silver. There are also the porcelain and glass rooms, as well
as rare coins, medals, miniatures, jewels and spectacular furniture, besides the
expected historic artifacts in gold and precious stones. Also stored are many
ancient documents and books, all of the highest quality and provenance.
The huge, covered Great Court is not to be missed, providing a walk-through
access and lined with galleries on its several floors. There is also a good
reproductions shop.

Mayfair

Old Bond Street and its extension, New Bond Street, run north to Oxford Street, leading to its famous shops and galleries. Note the famous and fashionable Liberty's department store on Regent Street, built in the 19th century. Smart shops throughout this area offer period pictures, furniture of English and Continental origin, fine tapestries and carpets, with some shops specializing in Oriental stock. New Bond Street itself is an especially prolific shopping thoroughfare, with its high-end shops and galleries. This street is home to Sotheby's, the giant multinational auction house, but it is also littered with smaller, more specialized shops that make for fun and lucrative browsing.

Adrian Alan

66-67 South Audley Street, W1 * 020 7495 2324 * www.adrianalan.com * Tube: Bond Street; Bus: 148 * Mon–Fri 09:30—18:30

Antique shop: Georgian and 19th-century furnishings, clocks, barometers, sculptures, bronzes

South Audley Street is one of the smartest in Mayfair, leading up from just above Piccadilly, and heading north to Grosvenor Square and the American Embassy. There is a range of smart shops, from fashion to florist, in and around this thoroughfare, but most importantly, there are some fine antiques establishments, so a long and slow walk is worthwhile. At Adrian Alan the special focus is on Continental, Georgian and 19th-century furnishings, including a range of clocks and barometers. There are also sculptures, bronzes and a host of decorative items to be found here. Transport, shipping and insurance are organized for customers if required.

The Amber Centre

24 St Christopher's Place, W1 * 020 7486 2998 * www.ambercentre.com * Tube: Bond Street; Bus: 6, 23, 94, 139 * Mon–Fri 19:30—17:00

Modern shop: old amber, gold and silver jewellery

A walk from Oxford Street to Wigmore Street along the narrow pedestrian passage called St Christopher's Place is a real pleasure. You will find lots of browsing here, with small shops of most kinds to look at, though no antique ones. However, you can buy old amber at this small modern shop, along with some gold and silver jewellery. A small section of the shop shows necklaces and ornaments of the late 19th and early 20th centuries, when these mysterious golden beads, often large and dramatic, were a popular choice for the 'artistic' or society woman.

Blüthner Piano Centre Ltd

1 Davies Street, W1 * 020 7753 0533 * www.bluthner.co.uk * Tube: Bond Street; Bus: 8 * Mon–Fri 09:00–17:30, Sat 10:00–17:00

Shop: new and antique pianos

In a long, green, carpeted salon, gleaming grand pianos flap their polished wings, though not all are new: some are 'antique', old and remodelled. The shop will pack and ship, too. Piano lessons are available for both beginners and more accomplished players.

The Bond Street Antiques Centre

124 New Bond Street, W1 * 020 7351 5353 * Tube: Bond Street; Bus: 6, 23, 94, 139 * Mon–Sat 10:00–18:00

Arcade of small shops: watches, porcelain, Oriental antiques, jewellery

This centre enjoys the reputation of being one of London's finest for antique jewellery, silver and objets d'art. Once you have found the narrow entrance, you will come upon a two-level arcade housing 30 small shops. The varied specialities include watches, porcelain, glass, Oriental antiques and jewellery.

Brian Haughton Antiques

3b Burlington Gardens, Old Bond Street, W1 * 020 7734 5491 * www.haughton.com * Tube: Green Park; Bus: 14 * Mon–Fri 10:00–17:00, Sat by appointment

Antique shop: Antique ceramics, 18th- and early 19th-century English and Continental pottery and porcelain

The porcelain lover will be in heaven here, for some of the finest schools, English and Continental, and especially Bow and Meissen, are on sale here, and beautifully displayed, too. A small modern shop with a wide window so you can see the stock easily, the standard is high, with some rare examples of decorated dinner sets showing the 18th-century potter's art. There are figurines, and an assortment of animals in porcelain. Sets of period drinking glasses, mostly Georgian, are a specialty, as are decanters. Charming, knowledgeable service, and a warm welcome.

David Aaron Ancient Art

22 Berkeley Square, London W1 * 020 7491 9588 * e-mail: davidaaron@hotmail.com * Tube: Green Park; Bus: 14 * Mon–Fri 09:00–18:00

Gallery: a range of Ancient Greek, Roman, Islamic and Egyptian art

This large-windowed, well-lit corner gallery faces the wide expanse of the famous square with its venerable lime trees. The ancient arts displayed here against the plain walls are of considerable quality, from sculptures to textiles. There are fine Greek, Roman and Egyptian marbles that could turn your home into a museum — though some, such as a draped Grecian goddess, would need plenty of space to be seen properly. There's a good deal of terracotta, pottery and smaller pieces too. Mr Aaron also specializes in Islamic arts, and a range of framed pieces and antique carpets is laid out.

Dix Noonan Webb

16 Bolton Street, W1 * 020 7016 1700 * www.dnw.co.uk * Tube: Green Park; Bus: 14 * Mon–Fri 09:00–18:00 * Check the website or catalogue for auction dates and viewing times

Auctioneers and valuers: coins, medals, paper money

Set in a one-block-long street just off Piccadilly, this firm of specialist auctioneers and valuers of all types of coins, medals and paper money claims to be the leading numismatic auction house in Britain. Many important collections are sold here; their auctions have handled 18 Victoria Crosses at the time of publication. Catalogue available in print as well as online. Free valuations offered.

Collectable coins, medals and currency are auctioned at Dix Noonan Webb.

Dover Street Market

17-18 Dover Street, W1 * **020 7518 0680** * **Tube: Green Park; Bus: 14** * **Mon–Sat 11:00–18:00 (19:00 on Thursdays)**

Market: fashions, jewellery, Victorian and Edwardian taxidermy

This new market in a recycled building is mostly occupied by fashions, jewellery and oddities. Among these are the antique items provided by Emma Hawkins. This Scottish dealer has an eye for the bizarre, and is represented with her wares in cases on all six floors. Many are taxidermy items such as stuffed birds, fish and animals displayed in glass bubbles and boxes. All are Victorian or Edwardian, the heyday of stuffing: you couldn't trade in these items now. Weird pieces include lamps made from zebra legs, and nasty-looking dogs on cushions.

Emanouel Corporation (UK) Ltd

64 South Audley Street, W1 * **020 7493 4350** *
www.emanouel.net * **Tube: Marble Arch; Bus: 148** *
Mon–Fri 10:00 – 17:30, Sat by appointment

Antique shop: 19th-century furnishings, porcelain, pottery, paintings

A considerable range of antiquities here. On show among a specialist selection of furnishings of the 19th century are clocks and glass, Oriental porcelain and pottery, paintings in oil, silver, and Islamic works of art. The firm specializes in buying on commission, with many clients deemed 'high profile'.

E. & R. Cyzer

33 Davies Street, W1 * **020 7629 0100** * **www.cyzerart.com** *
Tube: Bond Street; Bus: 6, 23, 94 * **Mon–Fri 10:00 – 17:00,**
or by appointment

Art gallery: 20th-century European and British paintings; exhibitions held

If you believe a dining room should be simple, chaste and dedicated to the pleasure of eating, then a sideboard, an antique table and chairs and a fine painting glowing on a plain wall will make that room very special. When Richard Cyzer set up this important gallery recently, its attraction was its choice of works to suit domestic interiors using a specific period of European and British painting, all of the 20th century. The accent is on masters of the early years, including Vlaminck, van Dongen, Chagall, Degas and Léger. Three special exhibitions are held each year.

Francis Kyle Gallery

9 Maddox Street, W1 * **020 7499 6870** *
www.franciskylegallery.com * **Tube: Oxford Circus; Bus: 6,**
12, 23, 88, 94 * **Mon–Fri 10:00 – 18:00, Sat 11:00 – 17:00**

Art gallery: a variety of styles; historic exhibitions

There are a great many art galleries in this fashionable area, especially along nearby Cork Street, but not all are as well organized and stylishly directed as this one. Francis Kyle maintains a corps of 35 artists, most of them long term, and all are represented here in a variety of styles. There are in fact six floors of pictures. The gallery also hosts important historic exhibitions. A warm welcome and well informed help here.

The Graham Gallery

60 South Audley Street, W1 * **020 7495 3151** * www.thegrahamgallery.com * **Tube: Bond Street; Bus: 148** * **Mon–Fri 10:00 – 18:00**

Gallery: 19th- and early 20th-century furniture

A family-run enterprise, this gallery is especially well known for Art Déco furniture and works of art, lighting, mirrors, sculpture and bronzes.

Grays Antique Markets

58 Davies Street, W1 * **020 7499 6260** * www.graysantiques.com * **Tube: Bond Street; Bus: 6 , 23, 94, 139, 189** * **Mon–Fri 10:00 – 18:00**

Antique market: antique jewellery, vintage fashion, toys and collectables

Handily situated near Oxford Street, this is a place for specialists. Grays is divided into two parts: the Grays section, in Davies Street, occupies a handsome Victorian building close to Bond Street Tube, and there are two levels within. Wares include jewellery, watches and 'small antiques'. The other part of Grays is just around the corner, and is called The Mews. This is the place for carpets, textiles, costumes, old toys and games, Art Nouveau and Art Déco, paintings and prints. The Mews is also known for housing Biblion, a showcase of over 150 dealers of antiquarian books, as well as Vintage Modes, selling vintage clothing, accessories and textiles.

Some shops of note in the Grays section include **Austin's Antiques**, at stand 137, which sells a range of small-sized Chinese and Japanese ceramics. **David Bowden**, at 107, offers Chinese, Japanese and other Oriental art objects. **Brian & Lynn Holmes**, at stand 304-6, sell Georgian and Victorian gold and silver jewellery, with the speciality of Scottish agate stones in settings. **The Jewellery Exchange** at 225 specializes in cameos and early 19th-century jewellery. **Shapiro & Co**, at 380, offers jewellery, silver, works of art and Russian items. For a change of pace, check out **Star Signings**, where you'll find sports memorabilia and autograph letters from famous personalities.

THE GILDED LILY

Grays Antiques Market, Stand No 145-146 ✱ **020 7499 62608**
✱ **www.graysantiques.com** ✱ **Mon–Fri 10:00 – 17:30**

This open-sided stand, with counters along its length, is unusually large, occupying (for these tiny premises) quite a wide, two-sided corner site on the lower ground floor of the market. Otherwise this is a typical example of these boutiques, each having its own speciality and style. Draw up one of the tall chairs and peruse the treasure trove of unusual 19th- and early 20th-century jewellery to be discovered here. There is a good selection of 9-carat gold from around the turn-of-the-century, with a particular interest in the post-war period.

The Gilded Lily is just one of the many specialist stands at Grays Antique Markets.

John Jaffa Antiques (The Antique Enamel Company Ltd)

340 Linen Hall, 162-168 Regent Street, W1 * 020 7434 3790 *
www.antique-enamels.co.uk * Tube: Piccadilly Circus, Oxford
Circus; Bus: 6, 12, 23, 88 * By appointment only

Small boutique: old enamels, perfume bottles, objets de vertu

This small space is for those who enjoy acquiring tiny articles, for it is crammed full
of intriguing and immaculate objects. Obviously the accent is on old enamels, with
lots of English and European examples. Not the most welcoming shop, but the
expertise is evident, and you may learn a lot. Other items for sale are varied, and they
range from perfume bottles, snuff and gold boxes to objets de vertu.

Biblion, housed in The Mews, is a must-visit destination for bibliophiles.

D. S. Lavender (Antiques) Ltd

26 Conduit Street, W1 * **020 7629 1782** * **e-mail: dslavender@clara.net** * **Tube: Bond Street; Bus: 6, 12, 23, 88** * **Mon–Fri 09:30 – 17:00**

Shop: fine jewels, miniatures and objets d'art

A small show window above a fake clipped hedge reveals one of the shop's strong points: many and varied antique seals once used to impress their owners' details in sealing wax. Inside, small items are shown against sea-blue satin display boxes. The cluster of miniatures is of special interest: from the 17th and 18th up to the early 19th centuries, there is a dazzling array of tiny portraits, some framed in jewels. Art Nouveau and Art Déco rings and brooches are on offer as well. Photos on the wall show Princess Diana visiting the stand at Grosvenor Fair.

Liberty Department Store

214-220 Regent Street, W1 * **020 7734 1234** * **Tube: Oxford Circus; Bus: 6, 12, 25, 88, 94** * **Mon-Sat 10:00 – 19:00, Thurs 10:00 – 21:00, Sun 12:00 – 18:00**

Antique departments: furniture from the Art Nouveau and Arts and Crafts periods, along with contemporary examples; small Russian oils and Japanese prints

There are two antique departments in this elegant old department store. The Fourth Floor has pieces grouped under the theme of 1850–1950, which means right up to early Danish designs. Most are 19th century however, with many Art Nouveau pieces associated with the style that Liberty set when it was founded. Examples from various schools are for sale, including Aesthetic and Arts and Crafts. Items include embossed silver plates, copper-framed mirrors, grillwork, and Clarice Cliff and Susie Cooper tea and coffee sets. Designers include Archibald Knox and Arthur Gaskin. Descriptive books of the periods are also available. A discerning selection of contemporary furniture and lighting is for sale here, too. Pleasant, friendly help is on hand. Downstairs on the lower ground floor is a charming gallery of small Russian oils and Japanese prints from around 1900, also well worth a visit.

Linda Wrigglesworth

34 Brook Street, W1 * 020 7408 0177 *
www.lindawrigglesworth.com * Tube: Chancery Lane;
Bus: 25, 242, 341 * By appointment only

Shop: Eastern antiquarian costumes, Oriental textiles, modern fashions

A unique shop specializing in antiquarian costumes from China, Korea and Tibet,
including robes, shoes and hats. Other Oriental textiles, costumes and wallhangings
are sold here as well. A new fashion line has recently been developed, and this shop
now sells an 'art to wear' modern fashion collection.

Mallett

141 New Bond Street, W1 * 020 7499 7411 *
www.mallettantiques.com * Tube: Bond Street;
Bus: 6, 23, 94, 139 * Mon–Fri 09:00 – 18:00

Grand department store: furniture, glass, 18th-century paintings

A splendid shop in the grand style of this noted street address. Five floors of rare
pieces grace their wide-windowed premises, first opened in 1810. Great English
antiques are their stated interest, and the grandest examples are all in immaculate
order: these include stellar Georgian chairs, tables and chests, and such rarities as
gilded book cases and lustrous marquetry commodes. Also stocked are prime French,
Irish and Italian pieces, along with glass items. Also for sale are 18th-century paintings, as well as bibelots, boxes, chandeliers and walking sticks.

Mansour Gallery

46-48 Davies Street, W1 * 020 7491 7444 * e-mail:
mail@mansourgallery.com * Tube: Bond Street;
Bus: 6, 23, 94 * Mon–Fri 09:30 – 17:30

Gallery: Greek statues, Roman nudes, Islamic art

Ancient art may need a deep pocket, yet it is undoubtedly the ultimate antique.
Modern and airy this space may be, but this venerable gallery has been at this same
location for 35 years. Step from marble-flagged pavement onto glossy wooden floors
surrounded by warm, dove-grey walls, a fine foil for the antiquities on show,

from Greek statues in rippling robes to Roman nudes. However, the preferred art of the owner is Islamic, and there are plenty of good examples here, from pots to platters and vases gleaming with bright decorations.

Marks Antiques

49 Curzon Street, W1 ❋ **020 7499 1788** ❋ **www.marksantiques.com** ❋ **Tube: Green Park; Bus: 14, 148** ❋ **Mon–Fri 09:30 – 18:30, Sat 09:30 – 17:30**

Antique shop: 17th-, 18th- and 19th-century silver, Chinese exportware, jewellery

Curzon Street, which runs from Berkeley Square to Park Lane, was once lined with palatial town houses – only one still remains. There are several good shops in the area, including this one, with its superb 17th-, 18th- and 19th-century silver by some of the best-known silversmiths of their times; for example, Paul Storr, Paul de Lamerie, Hester Bateman and Elkington & Co. They also sell Russian silver, Chinese exportware and assorted items of jewellery.

Michael Lipitch

Based centrally in Mayfair, W1 ❋ **07730 954 347** ❋ **e-mail: michaellipitch@hotmail.com** ❋ **By appointment only**

Private collection: 18th-century French and English works of art, furnishings

'I know what I like, and I enjoy selling things that I really enjoy myself', says Mr Lipitch enthusiastically. He shows from his home, and invitations can be obtained by appointment to visit his very personal collection. Hence, this is a most unusual experience. He spends a good deal of time travelling, searching out fine old pieces of European furniture and decorative items, but specializes mostly in 18th-century French and English works of art, furnishings and antiquities. He also offers consultancy.

Partridge Fine Arts

144–146 New Bond Street, W1 ❋ **020 7629 0834** ❋ **www.partridgeplc.com** ❋ **Tube: Bond Street; Bus: 6, 23, 94, 139** ❋ **Mon–Fri 09:30 – 17:30, Sat 11:00 – 16:00**

Grandiose house: fine arts, furniture, oil paintings, prints

The firm moved here in 1944, and the house has a palatial air, from the circular marble entry to its sweeping stair, leading up to two more sales floors. In cases and on shelves, a glittering horde of treasures are on display, prime pieces of splendid furniture stand on the wide floors, and fine quality oils and prints are clustered on the walls. The firm specializes in English and French 18th-century furniture, Old Master paintings, and English and Continental silver. Despite its air of grandeur, the staff gladly welcome and assist you. Publications are issued, as are catalogues with pictures of recent acquisitions, so ask about registering any special interest you may have. Important exhibitions are occasionally held, with specific themes.

S. J. Phillips Ltd

**139 New Bond Street, W1 * 020 7629 6261 *
www.sjphillips.com * Tube: Bond Street; Bus: 6, 23, 94, 139 *
Mon–Fri 10:00 – 17:00**

Grandiose shop: antique silver

A doorman ushers you into this grandiose shop, a palace of pleasures to anyone who loves silver: indeed, this is claimed to be the finest collection of antique silver in the world, from coffee pots to coasters, candlesticks to chargers, some by famous designers. Unusual items are on show here too, such as silver Torah bell stands from Amsterdam. The items here are mostly English, going back to the 16th and 17th centuries. (The oldest treasures are in a room of their own at the back of the premises.) There are miniatures and snuffboxes, and antique and modern jewellery, too. The staff can discuss each piece with considerable knowledge.

Rare Jewellery Collections Ltd

**3rd Floor, 45-46 New Bond Street, W1 * 020 7499 5414 *
www.rarejewellerycollections.com * Tube: Bond Street;
Bus: 6, 23, 94, 139 * By appointment only**

Antique consultants : assembly of art collections for private clients

A special angle here: this firm buys up desirable items in order to create art collections for wealthy clients, both private and corporate, who want a ready-made array of treasures. They also sell jewellery and antique watches, and will source individual pieces of jewellery for clients. Restoration and valuation services.

47

Richard Green (Fine Paintings)

33 New Bond Street, W1 * **020 7499 5553** * **Tube: Bond Street; Bus: 6, 23, 94, 139** * **Mon–Fri 10:00–18:00, Sat by appointment**

Gallery: Old Masters paintings

Entering this gallery is a bit like entering a venerable public London institution and realizing that some of these remarkable paintings are actually for sale. Classic and beautiful Old Masters of fine quality are on offer — and mostly at the high prices one would expect. This gallery specializes in 18th- and 19th-century British marine and sporting paintings, portraits, and Impressionist and Post-Impressionist paintings. There are two other Richard Green galleries: at 147 New Bond Street, and at 30 Dover Street. These branches specialize in other schools of paintings.

Sibyl Colefax and John Fowler Ltd

39 Brook Street, London W1 * **020 7493 2231** * **www.colefaxantiques.com** * **Tube: Bond Street; Bus: 25, 242, 341** * **Mon–Fri 09:30–17:30**

Antique shop: furniture and decorative items

This is a renowned shop, and a very elegant one, too. Perhaps best known for its fabrics and wallpapers, the shop's decorating and antiques business continues to flourish. Stock includes 18th- to early 20th-century English and Continental furniture, pictures, mirrors and lamps, with an emphasis on decorative items.

The Sladmore Gallery

32 Bruton Place, W1 * **020 7499 0365** * **Tube: Green Park; Bus: 14** * **Mon–Fri 10:00–18:00**

Gallery: antique and modern animal sculptures in metal, mostly bronze

This two-floored gallery, with its white, dramatically lit walls, is hidden behind Bruton Street on Bruton Place. 'We like it that way, it means we get the clients willing to search us out'. A large grizzly bear is on the prowl at the entrance to the gallery, which is devoted to antique and modern animal sculptures of all sizes, from life-size to miniature. They hail mostly from Europe, especially France, and date from 1870. Note the large horse's heads. Almost everything is in metal, principally bronze, though some of the polished and patinated pieces look as if they have been created from stone.

Sotheby's

34-35 New Bond Street, W1 * 020 7293 5000 * www.sothebys.com * Tube: Bond Street or Green Park; Bus: 6, 23, 94, 139 * Mon–Fri 09:00 – 17:00. Other location: Hammersmith Road, W14 * 020 7293 5555 * Mon 09:00 – 20:00, Tues–Fri 09:00-17:00, Sun 12:00 – 17:00

Auction house: decorative and fine art; an enormous selection of antiques

Like Christie's (see page 57), this firm represents the pinnacle of auctioneering. A multinational giant, it sells virtually every kind of decorative and fine art, as well as an enormous selection of antiques, including art, books, sculpture, antiquities, silver, ceramics, glass, jewellery, furniture, musical instruments, clocks, cars and wine. Catalogues can be bought (or perused) online, and are shipped upon request a few days before each sale. Free valuations.

M. Turpin

27 Bruton Street, W1 * 020 7493 3275 * www.mturpin.co.uk * Tube: Bond Street; Bus: 14 * Mon–Fri 10:00 – 18:00, or by appointment

Antique shop: 18th- and 19th-century furniture, boxes, caskets, Oriental items, sculptures, bronzes

Many different and delightful antique objects catch the eye in this wide-windowed shop on a smart street just off Bond Street, north of Piccadilly. The furniture here is mostly Georgian, of the 18th and 19th centuries, and includes fine chandeliers, barometers, unusual clocks and large, swagged, gilt-framed mirrors. There are rare yet useful pieces here, from dining chairs to magnificent break-fronts. There is also a large collection of boxes and caskets in wood and precious metals. Oriental items, too, as well as works of art, including sculptures and bronzes. Valuations made.

Victor Arwas Gallery

3 Clifford Street, W1 * **020 7734 3944** *
www.victorarwas.com * Tube: Green Park; Bus: 14 *
Mon–Fri 11:00—18:00, Sat 11:00—14:00

Gallery: books, bronzes, jewellery, pottery, glassware

A warm welcome at this completely delightful 40-year-old gallery of books old and
new. With its palpable atmosphere, it feels as if you are stepping back into a studio
of its chosen period, from 1880 to the 1940s, with plenty of Art Nouveau and Art
Déco on show. The choice of fine period jewels, many Edwardian designs and silver-
mounted, shows considerable style in their selection. Fine period pottery, figurines,
glass vases and decorated decanters are also for sale.

Vigo Carpet Gallery Ltd

6a Vigo Street, W1 * **020 7439 6971** * e-mail:
vigo@btinternet.com * Tube: Piccadilly Circus; Bus: 6, 12, 14,
23, 88, 94 * Mon–Fri 10:00—18:00, Sat 11:00—17:00

Carpet shop: antique and new handmade carpets

Oriental handmade rugs and carpets, both new and antique, are on sale here. The
carpets come from all over the world, with an emphasis on those from Iran, Pakistan,
China and India. There is a special antique carpet collection, as well as new carpets
made with reference to old patterns. There is also a restoration and valuation
service.

Windsor House Antiques

23 Grafton Street, London W1 * **020 7659 0340** *
www.windsorhouseantiques.co.uk * Tube: Green Park; Bus: 6,
12, 14, 23, 88 * Mon–Fri 09:30—18:00, or by appointment

Antique shop: period dining furniture, bronzes, paintings, porcelains

If you are looking for a set of good period dining furniture, this is the place to head
for. 'We always carry at least twelve sets of antique dining chairs and a similar number of tables', say the owners. Along with this good general stock of antiques, there
are fine works of art here: bronzes, oils, watercolours and porcelains.

Zelli Porcelain

30a Dover Street, W1 * **020 7493 0203** * **www.zelli.co.uk** *
Tube: Green Park; Bus: 14 * **Mon–Fri 09:00 – 18:00,
Sat 10:00 – 16:00**

Antique shop: *ornamental porcelains*

'We rarely see genuine antique pieces here', explains the charming manageress of this new two-level shop crowded with porcelain figurines, animals, birds, dinner plates, bowls, small decorative dishes and vases. 'But they do come in, and we always have people asking for them'. The ornamental stock on show are all reproductions of classical works. But if you want a copy of good quality, try here. The copies are usually made at the original factories, such as Royal Copenhagen and Meissen. Restoration service available.

Services

Holloway White Allom Limited
43 South Audley Street, Grosvenor Square, W1 *
020 7499 3962 * **Mon–Sat 09:00 – 18:00, Thurs 09:00 – 19:00**

White Allom is an interiors and decorating company with a reputation for high quality work. Among other contacts, the company works with Timothy Long Restoration, specialist in antique decorative art restoration. Services include cabinet-work, polishing and preserving original patination, upholstering and covering frames with traditional materials, gilding, marquetry and timepiece reparation. They will also maintain large collections on an ongoing basis.

John Lewis Partnership
Oxford Street, W1 * **020 7629 7711** * **www.johnlewis.com** *
Tube: Oxford Circus; Bus: 9, 10, 94 * **Mon–Sat 09:00 – 19:00,
Thurs 09:00 – 20:00, Sun 12:00 – 18:00**

This multi-floored department store is useful for finding new fabrics for restoring and re-covering antique pieces. There's a service for upholstering here, too. If you are looking for chair or sofa coverings, their department on the 3rd floor is very large and well stocked for unique furnishing and drapery fabrics. They have a huge stock, including fine Italian and French fabrics. Don't neglect the remaindered section either, for odd lots. Lots of bargain stock ends, too, in a range of fabrics.

Piccadilly

This wide, straight avenue was once a specialist area, where shops sold a London peculiarity – piccadills, a sort of shirt front collar, made of fine cotton. The statue of Eros (dubbed the God of Love, but intended to be the Angel of Charity) is regarded by many as the centre of London, although Trafalgar Square and the statue of Charles I is the official point from which distances are measured. There are several notable shopping arcades in this area, including the Royal Academy, the elegant Burlington Arcade, and the Piccadilly and the Princes' arcades. Off Regent Street is the Royal Opera Arcade, a real architectural gem – though neighbouring New Zealand House has unfortunately blocked off several of its show windows.

J. H. Bourdon-Smith Ltd

24 Mason's Yard, off Duke Street, SW1 * 020 7839 4714 *
Tube: Piccadilly Circus; Bus: 14 * Mon–Fri 09:30 – 18:00

Antique shop: old silver, silver gilt, gold, cutlery

The window of this small shop gleams like a treasure cave. Splendid old silver here, from 17th-century to Edwardian, as well as spectacular examples in gold and silver gilt. The pieces on offer are mostly English, with some Irish and Scottish examples. There are sets of cutlery and other assorted items for the table, from salt cellars to pap boats and wine labels. Four catalogues are issued regularly.

The Burlington Arcade

51 Piccadilly, W1 * 020 7493 1764 *
www.burlington-arcade.co.uk * Tube: Piccadilly Circus; Bus:
6, 12, 14, 23 * Mon–Sat 09:00 – 18:00

Shopping arcade: antique jewellery, maps; modern fashion

From the day it first opened in 1819, Burlington Arcade has remained one of the premier London shopping areas, appealing particularly to fashion-conscious customers. In keeping with the original vision for the Arcade, modern shoppers can find both antique and modern jewellery, silverware, pewter, connoisseur writing materials, antique maps, Irish linen, and many more fashionable and unique items.

DANIEL BEXFIELD ANTIQUES
26 Burlington Arcade, W1 * 020 7491 1720 *
www.bexfield.co.uk

In this elegant, small shop's vitrines are silver, objects of vertu, and jewellery from the 17th to the 20th centuries. The hallmarked silver is mostly English, but Continental silver is sold here, too. Items range from tea services to cutlery. Sterling silver only; no silver plate is sold here. Valuations are carried out upon request.

MAP WORLD
25 Burlington Arcade, W1 * 020 7495 5377 *
www.map-world.com

Antique atlases and maps are for sale here. This shop supplies largely to museums, collectors and interior designers.

Frost and Reed

2-4 King Street, SW1 * 020 7839 4645 * e-mail:
newyork@frostandreed.co.uk * Tube: Green Park; Bus: 6, 12, 14, 23, 88, 94 * Mon–Fri 09:00 – 17:30

Gallery: 20th-century pictures, small bronzes

There's a museum-like, hushed atmosphere in this opulent space. A variety of pictures, many in gilt frames, as well as works on paper, are well-spaced, with an accent on sporting as well as general subjects, mostly of the 20th century. There is also a range of small bronzes of animal and horse subjects. There's a mailing list for those with specific arts interests, and a New York gallery at 21 East 67th Street.

Grace Tsumugi Fine Art Ltd

8 Duke Street, SW1 * 020 7930 9953 * e-mail: japaneseart @grace-tsumigi.co.uk * Tube: Green Park; Bus: 6, 12, 14, 23, 88, 94 * Mon–Fri 11:00 – 18:00

Gallery: scrolls, panels, Chinese furniture

An array of screens, scrolls and tumbling tassels on two levels, this is a shadowy and dramatically designed gallery of Oriental subjects. There are fabric panels and gilt framed pictures of the 19th and 20th centuries of Eastern subjects. Several fine pieces of Chinese furniture, statues and stone curios are on sale, too. The sculptures range from golden divinities to quizzical buddhas and animals, and they are cunningly presented against a dark maroon wallpaper. Spot-lit to give them an exotic look, they glow with Eastern mystery. Courteous service.

Harvey and Gore

33 Duke Street, W1 * 020 7839 4033 * www.harveyandgore.co.uk * Tube: Green Park; Bus: 6, 12, 14, 23, 88, 94 * Mon–Fri 09:30 – 17:00

Antique shop: sculptures, miniatures, jewellery, silver

If you like small, refined antique pieces, this is a really delightful collection. In fact, a plethora of easily portable pleasures abounds here, ranging from an array of ornate snuff and patch boxes and small sculptures in various materials to decorative miniatures and amusing antique oddities. There is also an innovative range of jewellery and silver on show, as well as Sheffield plate.

The Princes Arcade

Between Piccadilly and Jermyn streets * Tube: Piccadilly Circus; Bus: 6, 12, 23, 94 * Mon–Fri 09:30 – 18:00, Sat 10:00 – 16:00 * Mon–Fri 09:30 – 17:00

Shopping arcade: rare books, paintings, chocolates, shirts

While not as select as the Burlington Arcade across the street, this arcade is still impressive, with over 40 small stores in a covered walkway dating from the 1800s. The shops here are devoted to rare books and fine paintings, chocolates and shirts.

NIGEL MILNE
Princes Arcade, 38 Jermyn Street, SW1 * 020 7434 9343 * www.nigelmilne.co.uk

A range of modern and classical designs and antique pieces from the Victorian and Edwardian eras. There is also a collection of silver gift items, and a design service.

St James's

Long the domain of the wealthy and influential, St James's still has some narrow courts and alleys to explore amidst the more modern buildings. The wide thoroughfare is the home of several London gentlemen's clubs (as is nearby Pall Mall), and it leads down to St James's Palace. Try Crown Passage leading from Pall Mall to King Street, and turn at the end to find the auction rooms occupied by Christie's. And be sure to take a stroll down Jermyn Street, where world-class tailors sit side by side with formidable antique shops and galleries.

Berry Bros & Rudd Ltd

3 St James's Street, London SW1 * 020 7396 9600 *
www.bbr.com * Tube: Green Park; Bus: 6, 12, 14, 23, 88, 94 *
Mon–Fri 10:00–18:00, Sat 10:00–16:00

Berry Bros & Rudd is one of the oldest and best wine merchants in Britain.

Jewellery for sale at The Silver Fund includes modern Danish designs.

Shop: vast selection of wines; malt whiskies, armagnacs, rums

The decor of this London shop has changed little since the company was established in 1698. The shop front is one of the few surviving 18th-century examples in London, and is worth a visit for a look alone. Hundreds of wines are sold here, from the everyday to the finest and the rarest. Experienced staff are there to guide you through the offerings. The Still Room houses a fine range of malt whiskeys, armagnacs and rums, including collectors' items. Online catalogue and shop.

Christie's

8 King Street, SW1 * 020 7839 9060 * www.christies.co.uk * Tube: Green Park; Bus: 8, 9, 14, 19, 22, 38 * Mon–Fri 09:00 – 17:00. Other location: 85 Old Brompton Road, SW7 * 020 7930 6074 * www.christies.co.uk * Tube: South Kensington; Bus: 14, 22, 49, 70, 74 * Check website for opening hours

Salesrooms: over 65,000 lots of all manner of items

The salesrooms at both locations hold frequent auctions of antiques and art: 210 auctions are held annually, offering over 65,000 lots. Viewing days tend to be held four days prior to an auction.

Peter Dale Ltd

11-12 Royal Opera Arcade, Pall Mall, SW1 * 020 7930 3695 * Tube: Piccadilly Circus; Bus: 6, 12, 14, 23, 88 * Mon–Fri 09.30 – 17:00

Antique shop: antique arms and armour

This shop specializes in antique arms and armour, and is said to be London's oldest established dealers of such. Situated in the Royal Opera Arcade, one of the oldest arcades in London.

The Silver Fund

The Silver Fund, 1 Duke of York Street, SW1 * 020 7839 7664 * www.thesilverfund.com * Tube: Piccadilly Circus; Bus 6, 12, 14, 23 * Mon–Fri 09:30 – 17:30

Large shop: classic modern silverware

Classic modern silverware, and lots of it, mainly with a concentration of classic Georg Jensen: there's plenty of the Danish master's work to look over here. Anyone who is a lover of silver should come and visit these large premises, for here are many good pieces of the precious metal. They will also buy Georg Jensen silver.

Trevor Philip and Son

75a Jermyn Street, SW1 * 020 7930 2954 * www.trevorphilip.com * Tube: Piccadilly Circus; Bus: 6, 12, 14, 23 * Mon–Fri 09:30 – 18:00

Gallery: old scientific instruments

A handsome, wide-windowed, chastely decorated gallery, revealing lots of unusual treasures within – from large library globes and complicated orreries, to telescopes and magnifying glasses. The speciality here is old scientific instruments of all kinds. Here for over 20 years, this intriguing gallery also offers occasional stylish, different articles such as a set of Regency dining chairs, a Fornasetti desk, porcelains and unusual sculptures such as the terra cotta lion maintaining guard near the door. However, it was pointed out by the helpful manager that these items are subsidiary to the gallery's main scientific theme.

Weiss, the Gallery

59 Jermyn Street, SW1 * 020 7409 0035 * www.weissgallery.com * Tube: Piccadilly Circus; Bus: 6, 12, 14, 23 * Mon–Fri 10:00 – 18:00, or by appointment

Gallery: late Tudor period paintings

It's quite surprising how many important historic paintings are still in private hands. As they come up in auction rooms, they often then move on to be shown for sale in specialist galleries of London. Here the accent is on the late Tudor period (even offering a portrait of Elizabeth I), and 17th-century portraits too, often quite large and elaborate. This established firm moved to Jermyn Street in 2004, yet the wooden floors, good lighting and remarkable spaciousness help to retain a historic air, particularly with the richly tapestried walls in the two connected galleries.

Specialist shop Trevor Philip and Son sells a range of old scientific objects.

North London

North London is an immense area. Going up from Oxford Street you arrive at Marylebone, bordering the gorgeous Regent's Park. Alas, the surrounding streets once boasted some lovely antique shops, but not any more. Beyond the Euston Road is Camden Town which, like Chalk Farm, used to have some antique outlets, but now very few remain. The real antique centre in North London today is Islington, home to the famous Camden Passage Antiques Market, with its multiple shops and arcades. Moving northwest, it's a slow climb to Hampstead and its wide, wild heath boasting splendid views of London below.

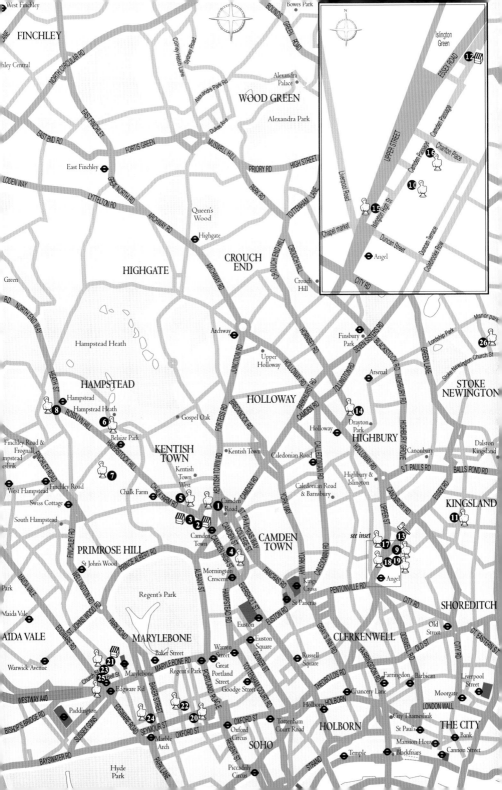

Camden Town

Named after Charles Pratt, the Earl of Camden, this part-residential, part-business conurbation is a lively place, with cafés, pubs, music venues and a busy High Street. It was developed after the arrival of the railways in 1830; Euston was the terminus for the London and Birmingham Railway. Charles Dickens referred to the area in *Dombey and Son*, but it did not become a smart place to live until quite recently. Today, the area is well known for its famous markets, popular on the weekends, and selling a variety of lifestyle, fashion and often bizarre goods, with the Stables Market offering an assortment of antique items. The Regent's Canal runs through the north end of the area, and makes for a lovely walk. Close by is Regent's Park, home of the London Zoo.

Art Furniture

158 Camden Street, London NW1 * 020 7267 4324 * www.artfurniture.co.uk * Tube: Camden Town; Bus: 24, 27, 29, 176 * Mon–Sun 12:00 – 17:00

Antique shop: furniture from the Arts and Crafts movement, metalware

All stock is original from the Arts and Crafts movement, by firms such as Liberty & Co, Shapland & Petter, Heals, Harris Lebus and Wylie and Lochead. Many pieces are by architects and designers such as Baillie-Scott, E.A. Taylor and George Walton. Metalwares by W.A.S. Benson, Keswick School of Industrial Art, and Newlyn are also stocked. Shipping can be arranged throughout the UK and worldwide. The shop plans on expanding its wares to include fine furniture from the Art Déco, Modernist and 1950s periods.

Camden Lock Market

Camden Lock Place, NW1 * 020 7284 2084 * www.camdenlock.net * Tube: Camden Town, Chalk Farm; Bus: 24, 27, 29, 31 134, * Many stalls open Sat–Sun 10:00 – 18:00; some stalls open weekdays

Market: *vintage clothing, Arab textiles, hand-carved sculpture, Indian jewellery*

Situated on the Regent's Canal, this original market is very popular on weekends. It was a timber yard until 1975, when the redundant space was opened as a market with alleys and open spaces. A multitude of wares in this space, including vintage clothing, Middle Eastern textiles, hand-carved sculpture and Indian jewellery.

Camden Stables Market

Off Chalk Farm Road, opposite the junction with Hartland Road, NW1 * www.camdenlock.net * Tube: Camden Town, Chalk Farm; Bus: 24, 27, 29, 31 134 * Most stalls open Mon–Sun 10:00 – 18:00

Market: *vintage clothing, antique furniture, collectables*

This market is a good bet, with its 350-odd shops and stalls, all spread out among and under the arches of the North London Railway. All sorts of clothes and decorative items overflow in this London version of a Paris 'flea market', with some bizarre stuff, too. Bargains are the main attraction, with lots of vintage clothing items, from beaded dresses to ancient shoes. The 'Horse Hospital', a section of the market (located in an area formerly used to care for horses injured pulling canal barges), now houses around 40 shops selling antiques, furniture and collectables.

Reckless Records

92 Camden High Street, NW1 * 020 7387 1199 * www.reckless.co.uk * Tube: Mornington Crescent; Bus: 24, 27, 29, 88 * Mon–Fri 10:00 – 20:00, Sat–Sun 10:00 – 19:00

Large store: *vinyl discs, tapes, CDs*

Another branch of this large store for second-hand vinyl discs, tapes and CDs of all types of music. There is a 'rarities' section, as well as a 'classic vinyl' section. There is also an Islington branch of this shop (see page 78).

Chalk Farm

The wide main thoroughfare called Chalk Farm Road heads north from West London up towards Hampstead. As an old route it gained its name from the Chalk Farm public house, which had nothing to do with chalk but is corrupted from a long-ago farm family name. The area has gained some fame from the Roundhouse, originally a rail shed used for the early rail arrivals here, and subsequently a popular entertainment centre. Opposite is Marine Ices, widely considered one of the best ice-cream shops in London.

Chalk Farm Antiques

60 Chalk Farm Road, NW1 * 020 7267 1612 * Tube: Chalk Farm; Bus: 24, 168 * Tues–Sun 11:00 – 18:00

Antique shop: A range of antique country furniture

A shop specializing in French country antique furniture, dating from the early 1900s to the 1950s. They also offer a furniture painting and restoration service.

Services

W. R. Harvey & Co (Antiques) Ltd
70 Chalk Farm Road, NW1 * 01933 706 501 * www.wrharvey.co.uk * Tube: Chalk Farm; Bus: 24, 168 * By appointment only

Workshop: the restoration of antiquities

This is a firm that has specialized in the restoration of antiquities for over 40 years. All aspects of period restoration are undertaken, even for museum collections. Special skills listed as offered in their workshops include general cabinet-making, the repairing and replacing of inlay and the delicate and rare woods of marquetry work, traditional (and French) polishing, general upholstery and leather lining of desks and period boxes.

Hampstead

Together with Highgate, this desirable residential area is known as 'Village London'. The area has a good deal of historical interest, especially of the literary and artistic kinds. Past inhabitants include John Keats and Dr Samuel Johnson; their dwellings are marked with blue plaques. The many small shops and galleries of Hampstead are laced with fashion outlets, restaurants and bars. There are a few good antique venues, several of which are housed in private abodes, to be visited 'by appointment'. After shopping, the Heath makes for a heady walk; you'll feel worlds away from the noisy city.

Tony Bingham

11 Pond Street, NW3 * 020 7794 1596 * www.oldmusicalinstruments.co.uk * Tube: Belsize Park; Bus: 46, 268 * Mon–Fri 10:30—17:30

Music shop: all things to do with musical instruments

If you needed any more assurance that Hampstead is a musical place, then here's another shop offering objects of interest with a music theme. Almost anything to do with musical instruments is sold here. There are books on music, both old and new, and many antique musical instruments as well. There are also oil paintings, watercolours, photographs and engravings with the same subject in mind. Established over 40 years ago, Mr Bingham's passion is evident. After visiting this shop, make a complementary visit to nearby Fenton House (see page 68) to view its fine collection of old instruments.

Brendan J. O'Brien

PO Box 7562, NW3 * 020 7431 3519 * Viewing by appointment only

Antique shop: 18th- and 19th-century English and French furniture

There is some very fine English and French furniture here. There is the odd 17th-century piece, but most are 18th and 19th century, accented with accessories and framed engravings and prints. There are some Asian works of art for sale as well.

Otto Haas (A. and M. Rosenthal)

49 Belsize Park Gardens, NW3 * 020 7722 1488 * e-mail: contact@ottohaas-music.com * Tube: Belsize Park; Bus: 268 * By appointment Mon–Fri, closed Sat

Music shop: printed material on all kinds of music

Very long established (since 1866), this business, located on an attractive Hampstead street, is a place dedicated to printed material on all kinds of music. Manuscripts, letters, autographs and rare books pertaining to music are offered.

Hampstead Antique and Craft Emporium

12 Heath Street, NW3 * 020 7794 3297 * e-mail: hampsteademporium.co.uk * Tube: Hampstead; Bus: 268, 603 * Tues–Fri 10:30 – 17:00, Sat 10:00 – 18:00, Sun 11:30 – 17:30

Shopping arcade: specialist dealers in Art Déco glassware and perfume bottles, jewellery, crystal vases

This attractive arcade is narrow, like an old street, making use of a back passage (well marked, running down off 12 Heath Street), and containing 24 pocket-sized shops. There you'll find experienced dealers specializing in 1930s Art Déco glassware, jewellery, lighting, pictures, crystal vases and Art Déco perfume bottles.

RECOLLECTIONS ANTIQUES
Hampstead Antique and Craft Emporium, 12 Heath Street, NW3 * 020 7431 9907 * e-mail: juneatlantiques@aol.com

Blue-and-white 19th-century ware, glass, simple country-style 19th-century furniture, children's toys and antique kitchen equipment are sold here.

COLIN SMITH
Hampstead Antique and Craft Emporium, 12 Heath Street, NW3 * 07976 693 581

The genial and helpful Mr Smith is a collector of curiosities, and his small courtyard shop is fascinating, literally filled with objects of interest, from cutlery to small antiques of all kinds.

Old instruments, musical scores and books are abundant at Tony Bingham.

While you're in the area...

THE COLLECTION AT KENWOOD HOUSE

Hampstead Lane, NW3 * 020 8348 1286 * Tube: Archway, Golders Green; Bus: 210 * Open every day 11:00 – 17:00 * Free admission

On the heights of Hampstead Heath, this museum offers many treasures, as well as wide views of London from its gardens. The great architect Robert Adam worked on the house in the 1770s for his patron the Earl of Mansfield, who was the Lord Chief Justice of the day. At that time Neo-classical was the flavour of the age, and Adam reigned supreme – not only was he responsible for the reconstruction of the house, but he also designed the splendid furniture here, some of it made by his contemporary, master-maker Thomas Chippendale. There are also some spectacular oil paintings on show.

FENTON HOUSE

Windmill Hill, Hampstead, NW3 * 020 7435 3471 * www.nationaltrust.org * Tube: Hampstead; Bus: 102, 226 * Check the website for opening times * Admission fee

A small and elegant one-time Georgian family home. Built of warm red brick with a classical 18th-century facade, Fenton House (now a National Trust property) has a collection of antique and rare musical instruments – most of which are in working order – assembled in its handsomely panelled principal rooms. The home also contains an outstanding collection of porcelain, 17th-century needlework pictures and Georgian furniture. A delightful walled garden and a working kitchen garden are also on site.

Islington

Renowned for its busy street and social life, smart restaurants and many theatres, fashionable Islington is a lively, lived-in place with some fine architecture, too. The central Angel tube station commemorates a 13th-century inn that stood here at a crossroads marking one of the main entries to London, down which cattle and poultry were herded daily for the consumption of its citizens. But this area is not just a series of busy thoroughfares; it is also an interesting and lively centre for visitors, with an important antique market and many excellent antique shops and stands.

The African Waistcoat Company

33 Islington Green, N1 * 020 7704 9698 *
www.africanwaistcoatcompany.com * Tube: Angel; Bus: 4, 19, 20, 38, 43, 56, 73 * Wed–Sat 10:00–16:00, Sun 10:00–14:00

Shop: vintage African fabrics

Stylish and colourful waistcoats from West Africa may sound an odd antique item, but here in this pocket-size shop are some remarkable vintage fabrics in original makes and designs, many of them old. Used to make up fashionable garments at London tailor shops, '…all are hand-woven, locally designed fabrics. I also have for sale African jewellery and ornaments', says the genial owner. He is happy to chat about his unique fabrics, often in atypical colours and derived from classic Nigerian designs.

Angel Arcade

116 Islington High Street, Camden Passage, N1 *
Tube: Angel; Bus: 4, 19, 20, 38, 43, 56, 73 *
Wed 07:30–17:00, Sat 09:00–17:30

Antique arcade: a range of shops selling a wide variety of antiques

You'll find all sorts of decorative and general antiques here, from majolica ceramics to Venetian mirrors. A 20th-century lighting specialist and an antique-doll dealer are also on the premises, and primitive and folk art can be had here, too.

ARGOSY ANTIQUES
**Shop 4, Angel Arcade, Camden Passage, N1 * 020 7359 2517
* Wed & Sat 07:00 — 16:30, Thurs & Fri 10:00 — 15:00**

A shop specializing in antique lighting, door furniture, silver, silver plate and Sheffield plate. Bronzes too, including samples from Vienna, circa 1840-1920.

KATE BANNISTER ANTIQUES
**Shop C, Angel Arcade, Camden Passage, N1 * 0207 704 6644
* e-mail: kateebannister@aol.com * Wed & Sat 07:30 — 16:30**

A charming shop selling decorative antiques, including tramp art, twig and bamboo furniture, lighting, inkwells, papier mache and antler and horn accessories.

VAL COOPER ANTIQUES
**Shop E, Angel Arcade, Camden Passage, N1 * 020 7226 4301
* e-mail:valcooperantique@aol.com * Wed & Sat 07:30 — 16:30**

An interesting variety of offerings, including bamboo furniture, majolica, papier mache, brass frames, Black Forest carvings and decorative accessories.

The Antique Trader

85-87 Southgate Road (7 Millenium Works), N1 * 020 7359 2019 * www.millineryworks.co.uk * Tube: Highbury; Bus: 76, 141 * Tues–Sat 11:00 — 18:00, Sun 12:00 — 17:00

Antique shop: late 19th-century furnishings and fabrics, brass, pottery

This is a shop with a speciality: that unusual period of the late 19th century, when the Arts and Crafts movement started up in London. The movement was dominated by artists and architects, and its unique style quickly became fashionable. Additional interests in brass and pottery items. No reproductions.

Camden Passage Antiques Market

Camden Passage, off Upper Street, N1 * www.camdenpassageantiques.com * Tube: Angel; Bus: 4, 19, 20, 38, 43, 56, 73 * Most antique shops are open Wed 07:00 — 14:00 and Sat 08:00 — 16:00. Books and prints on sale Thurs 07:00 — 16:00

Antique market: Antiques of all kinds housed in an array of arcades, markets and shops

The term 'Camden Passage' refers to a small section of the greater Islington area. Created in 1766, it has retained much of its charm, despite having been bombed during World War II. The first antique market appeared here in the 1960s, and since then it has become a prolific antique centre, housing a mixture of permanent shops, malls, and stalls, as well as those selling their wares from the pavement. The range of items for sale is extensive, and includes Georgian, Victorian and Continental furniture; English and Oriental porcelain and pottery, fine antique silver, Art Nouveau and Art Déco items, art pottery, barometers, bronzes, chandeliers, clocks, commemoratives, dolls, games, kitchenalia, jewellery, lighting, mirrors, musical boxes, paintings, prints, scientific instruments, silver-plate, textiles, toys, vintage fashion: the list goes on! There are over 300 dealers in Camden Passage. The three best-known arcades are the Angel Arcade (see page 69), the Mall Antiques Arcade (see page 76), and the Pierrepont Arcade (see page 77).

THE FURNITURE VAULT (JONATHAN JAMES)
50 Camden Passage, N1 * 020 7704 8266 * Wed & Sat 09:00 – 17:00

Occupying a corner with large windows, this big, open and imposing space is suitable for the range of mostly 19th- and early 20th-century pieces it shows: many of them are massive in true Victorian taste. Among examples always on show are big leather armchairs, desks, imposing sideboards, bookcases, large dining tables and sets of chairs. On display as well are suitable period ornaments. Appropriately, the shop has an Edwardian feeling, with the stock set against dark green walls.

ORIGIN
25 Camden Passage, N1 * 020 7704 1326 * www.origin101.co.uk * Wed & Sat 10:00 – 6:00, Thurs & Fri 12:00 – 6:00

A neat and smartly minimal shop, offering furnishings and decorative objects of the 20th century. Scandinavian modernism is accented here, with a number of pieces suitable to be cited as design stars of their era, many from the revival of simple telling styles of the fifties and sixties, such as metal-made, moulded chairs. The 'new' examples here were, and are, classics, especially the Scandinavian furnishings, with a decided slant towards the one-time fashionable and distinctive Danish teak. The 'new look' extends to handsome brushed steel or silver cutlery, tableware and fabrics of this emerging time.

KEVIN PAGE ORIENTAL ART
4 Camden Passage, N1 * 020 7226 8558 *
www.kevinpage.co.uk * Wed–Sat 10:00 – 17:00

This small gallery stands at the entry to the Passage. Here you will find, in a variety of sizes, rare, framed images of China and Japan in a parade of rare and unusual prints and original works dating from the 17th, 18th and 19th centuries, with an emphasis on the Japanese Meiji period. Complementing the many pictures in stock is an array of Oriental porcelains; the focus is on Satsuma, Chinese and Japanese decorative ceramics.

TEMPUS ANTIQUES
13 Camden Passage, N1 * 020 7359 9555 *
www.tempusantiques.com * Tues–Sat 10:00 – 16:00

Specializing in French mantle clocks circa 1790-1880, including garnitures and singles, and Bronze d'oré with Sèvres panels. There is also a selection of British, Dutch and French tall clocks circa 1730-1900. French credenza cabinets in walnut and mahogany are also sold.

JAN & CAROLE VAN DEN BOSCH
Shop 1, Georgian Village, Camden Passage, N1 * 020 7226 4550 * Wed & Sat 08:00 – 16:00, or by appointment

Silver and jewellery from the Art Nouveau, Arts and Crafts, Jugendstil and Skonvirke movements are the emphasis here. Furniture, ceramics and glass from these periods are also for sale.

Carol Ketley Antiques
PO Box 16199, N1 * 020 7379 5529 * By appointment only

Antique shop: antique glass (mostly English)

Close to Camden Passage, here is a specialist in antique glass, most of which is English. Mirrors of various periods and decorative antiques are also for sale. The dedication and taste of Ms Ketley becomes obvious when you see what she offers. A range of decanters and sets of glasses are of a very high quality, often engraved, and sometimes decorated with incised designs. Decanters from the early 18th century are on show, mostly made from clear glass. Some are even available in pairs, a relative rarity. This dealer shows at major fairs.

Collectors of Oriental porcelains will find Kevin Page's wares enticing.

Criterion Auctioneers

53 Essex Road, N1 * 020 7350 5707 *
www.criterion-auctioneers.co.uk * Tube: Angel; Bus: 38, 56,
73, 341 * Auctions are held every Monday evening throughout
the year, starting late afternoon. Viewings (essential) are
frequent and take place at the following times: Fri 14:00 –
20:00; Sat & Sun 10:00 – 18:00; Day of sale from 10:00

Auction house: *antiques, decorative furnishings, small items*

This is an unusual place to find: a genuine local auction house selling antiques and
decorative furnishings as well as associated small items on a regular basis. Many
pieces for sale are sourced locally, and thus there are no themed sales as such.
Criterion has been established at this brick-fronted, single-storey property with its
red signboards for 15 years. Free valuations offered.

Intricate marquetry adorns some of the unique pieces at Dome Antiques.

Dome Antiques (Exports) Ltd

40 Queensland Road, N7 * 020 7700 6266
* www.domeantiques.com * Tube: Holloway Road;
Bus: 43, 153 * Mon–Fri 09:30 – 16:30, Sat & Sun by
appointment

Showrooms: desks, library and dining tables, decorative furniture

Established in 1961, there is a wide range of pieces in these extensive showrooms, mostly of the late 18th century: desks, library and dining tables, occasional tables; also sets of dining chairs and various kinds of cabinets and cupboards. There is a speciality in decorative furniture ranging from 1780 to 1900, too. In addition, the premises are open on weekdays for a service of high-quality traditional restoration, French polishing and upholstery. Other services include bespoke cabinet-making.

High-quality restoration work is performed at the Dome Antiques workshop.

The Mall Antiques Arcade

359 Upper Street, Camden Passage, N1 * **020 7351 5353** *
Tube: Angel; Bus: 4, 19, 30, 43, 56, 73 * **Wed 10:00–17:00,**
Sat 09:00 – 18:00

Antique arcade: two levels of shops selling a variety of antiques

This is one of the most interesting antique arcades in London, with over 35 dealers housed. Starting from the Angel tube station, go up and enter the modern three-level building beside the street to find lots of interesting little shops spaced along the Upper Mall, a sparkling clean and brightly lit indoor passage. Several of the shops deal in conventional stock, with plenty of jewellery and small figurines, but there are specialists as well. There are two selling levels here, and the downstairs Lower Mall has much more space, so there you will find bigger areas with a range of antique furniture on show at several shops. If you want a meal break, then on top of the arcade the airy and well-lit Lola's is worthwhile, a recommended restaurant of style with set lunch menus (tel 020 7359 1932).

COUNT ALEXANDER JEWELS
No 13 Upper Mall * **020 7354 0058** *
www.countalexander.com * **Tues–Fri 10:00 – 16:30,**
Sat 10:00 – 17:30

The antique business undoubtedly attracts characters, and here, at a crowded and glittering cranny of a shop, a tall, leather-clad and mustachioed artist shows a host of reproductions of the 'famous crown jewels' of Austria, England, France and Russia. All are on show, and include necklaces, chokers, rings, cravat pins, cufflinks and even jewelled bodice ornaments and shoe buckles. Some of his range of elegant tiaras can even be converted to necklaces. The artist hand-makes all of his wares, triple-plated with palladium, and sets them with Austrian Swarowski crystals and Russian cubic zirconian stones.

LEOLINDA
No 3 Upper Mall * **020 7226 3450** *
Wed & Sat 10:00 – 17:00

A charming shop, original in its style because Leolinda Costa is Portuguese and many of her wares come from her home country. Her specialist areas are ethnic jewellery and gemstones: she is fond of rubies, turquoise and old amber, and jewellery pieces made between 1890 and 1910. In her crowded, yet well-arranged, window there's an accent on Indian and Russian pieces as well as Portuguese. Hallmarked 19th-century silver settings and cameos can also be found here, as well as Art Nouveau glass. Although her stock ranges up to Art Déco, she also has some oddities such as old fabrics, veils and scarves.

PATRICIA BAXTER ANTIQUES
Nos 2 & 3 Lower Mall ❊ **020 7354 0886** ❊
e-mail: baxantique@aol.com ❊ **Wed & Sat 10:00 – 18:00**

A large downstairs unit shows mostly 18th- and 19th-century English plain 'middle range' furniture, with an accent on large, late-Georgian and Victorian dining tables and chairs, these handily 'dressed' with glasses and settings to show customers how they might look at home. There are also occasional chairs, massive 'Empire' sideboards, and superb chests-of-drawers of Continental origin, some with spectacular wood veneers. Lamps and lighting fixtures include glass chandeliers. Vases, mirrors and some pictures are also for sale. Helpful, knowledgeable assistance.

R. LALIQUE GLASS
No 27 Upper Mall ❊ **020 7226 6367** ❊ **e-mail:**
rlaliqueglass@btinternet.com ❊ **Wed & Sat 10:00 – 18:00**

A beautifully arranged and well-lit display of the classic late 19th- and into the 20th-century French glassware known as Lalique, a style and material that is instantly recognizable (it has soft, cloudy, pearly grey or pastel effects). Lalique was responsible not only for a beautiful range of Art Déco vases, bowls and many decorative items, but also for architectural lighting: pieces for restaurants, hotel foyers, showrooms and shops, such as large lamps, illuminated sculptures, staircase mouldings and so on. A range of vases by Gallet and other makers is also on show, and large illustrated books on French glass are for sale. Helpful and informed service.

Pierrepont Arcade
Camden Passage, N1 ❊ **Tube: Angel; Bus: 4, 19, 20, 43, 56, 73**
❊ **Most shops open Wed & Sat 07:00 – 15:00**

Antique arcade: photos, prints, ceramics, watches, jewellery

Built after a World War II bomb destroyed its predecessor, this arcade has a small covered area where dealers display their wares on tables. A series of shops surrounding the tables also form part of this arcade. Items for sale include old photos and prints, ceramics, toys, watches and jewellery.

MARCUS ROSS ANTIQUES
16 Pierrepont Arcade, Camden Passage, N1 * 020 7359 8494

This shop specializes in 19th-century Imari and Oriental porcelain. They have a large selection of 18th-century Chinese export porcelain, including blue and white platters and plates, Chinese Imari, Famille-Rose and related wares. Rose Medallion and other 19th-century decorative Chinese and Japanese porcelain is sold here, too. The stock changes often, say the owners, with new items arriving all the time.

SUGAR ANTIQUES
8-9 Pierrepont Arcade, Camden Passage, N1 * 020 7354 9896 * www.sugarantiques.com

A shop within the arcade specializing in vintage wrist watches (Rolex, Longines, Omega), pocket watches, classic fountain pens, lighters, small silver collectables and costume jewellery. Online catalogue.

Reckless Records

79 Upper Street, N1 * 020 7359 0501 * www.reckless.co.uk * Tube: Angel; Bus: 4, 19, 30, 43, 56, 73 * Mon–Fri 10:00–20:00, Sat & Sun 10:00–19:00

Large store: vinyl discs, tapes, CDs

The Islington branch of this large store for old vinyl discs, second-hand records, tapes and CDs also has a rarities section and a classic vinyl section. There is another branch of this store in Camden Town (see page 63).

Rockarchive Gallery

110 Islington High Street, N1 * 020 7704 0598 * www.rockarchive.com * Tube: Angel; Bus: 4, 19, 30, 43, 56, 73 * Tues–Sat 11:00–18:00, Sun 11:00–17:00

Gallery: recent history in photographs

Recent history here, with photographs of the latter half of the 20th century. An unusual and arresting gallery, this venue makes a dramatic statement, standing out among surrounding and very varied antiques shops. It's a fascinating display, as spot-lit pictures of rock singers, as well as concert, film and show celebrities, shine out in a handsome, modern, cinnamon-walled gallery. There are some general subjects too, but the pictures are mostly of film stars, some of which were snapped by the fellow-famous. For devotees and collectors of old black-and-white memorabilia photographs, this is a genuine heaven.

Tadema Gallery

10 Charlton Place, N1 * 020 7359 1055 *
www.tademagallery.com * Tube: Angel; Bus: 4, 19, 30, 43, 56,
73 * Wed & Sat 10:00 – 17:00, or by appointment

Gallery: late 19th- and early 20th-century jewellery

Specializing in late 19th- and early 20th-century jewellery, including Art Nouveau, Jugendstil, British Arts and Crafts and Art Déco through to artist-designed jewels circa 1960, this store won the coveted British Antiques and Collectables award in 2004.

Services

Michenuels of London Ltd
Unit 7, Titan Business Estate, Ffinch Street, Deptford, SE8 *
020 8694 9206 * www.michenuels.co.uk

It is rare to see the description 'French polishing' associated with the world of antiques – it is very much a 20th-century innovation, providing gleaming and silky wood surfaces, a process used only for modern articles as a rule. It's now much in demand for office furniture and fittings. Aside from this unique area of expertise, the firm also provides spray lacquer finishes, sanding and polishing, repairs, cleaning and maintenance as well as the restoration of furniture, staircases and hardwood floors, wood surroundings, parquet and panelling. Services are available for both individuals and professional companies. While Michenuels will soon no longer be based in Islington, they are happy to perform their specialized service anywhere in London, for companies or private individuals.

Marylebone

Once home to warrior monks, later a hunting preserve for Henry VIII, and eventually developed by James Gibbs, Marylebone stretches north from Oxford Street to Regent's Park, and is bounded by Great Portland Street and Edgware Road. Rural until the 18th century, the area is now largely residential, with quality Georgian architecture. The main artery, Marylebone High Street, has many interesting shops and restaurants, and Marylebone Road is home to Madame Tussaud's wax museum. For those in search of antiques, there is Alfie's, an important market, and various shops as well, all congregated on and around Church Street.

Alexander Furnishings, Curtain and Fabrics

51-61 Wigmore Street, W1 * 020 7935 7806 * Tube: Bond Street; Bus: 139, 189, 274 * Mon–Sat 09:00 – 18:00

Shop and workroom: curtain and furnishing fabrics, accessories

A treasure house for furnishing fabrics of almost every imaginable kind, this shop provides helpful and polite assistance. Both the shop and workroom, which occupy no fewer than six shop fronts along this elegant street, almost opposite the Wigmore Hall, are stuffed with rolls and bolts of fabric for curtains, coverings, cloths, much of it in unusual antique designs and colours, as well as velvet, embroidered silks or satins for chairs and sofas. Swags, tassels, curtain poles and other accessories are also available. Work is carried out on the premises, and estimates are provided for free.

Alfie's Antique Market

13–25 Church Street, NW8 * 020 7723 6066 * www.alfiesantiques.com * Tube: Marylebone; Bus: 6, 23, 27, 453 * Tues–Sat 10:00 – 18:00

Antique market: over a hundred dealers selling a range of antiques

A fabulous maze of treasures located in a historical street market on Church Street, Alfie's is home to 100 leading antiques dealers, and is where many dealers shop for their wares. The substantial range and quantity of stock includes traditional 18th- and 19th-century antiques, including antique cushions, advertising posters, silver, furniture, paintings and prints, jewellery, ceramics, and vintage clothing and accessories. There are also quite a few dealers selling items of mid-century modern design as well if you want to pick up some 'antiques of the future'. Competitive prices.

Blunderbuss Antiques

29 Thayer Street, W1 ＊ 020 7486 2444 ＊ www.blunderbuss-antiques.co.uk ＊ Tube: Bond Street; Bus: 6, 23, 94, 139, 189 ＊ Tues–Fri 09:30 — 16:30, Sat 09:30 — 16:00

Antique shop: military and naval

A small, old-fashioned shop, yet with its double-fronted red-framed windows showing a regular parade of military and naval items, it is definitely intriguing. Stock ranges from uniforms to weapons, and from pictures of ships and ship models to embossed plaques. Other wares include military, naval and air force items, from army officer caps with Victorian plumes and hackles, to drums and whole racks of swords and daggers. Also bobbies' helmets, solar topees — even army boots can be had here.

Cristobal

26 Church Street, NW8 ＊ 020 7724 7230 ＊ www.cristobal.co.uk ＊ Tube: Edgware Road; Bus: 6, 16, 98, 139, 189 ＊ Tues–Sat 10:00 — 17:00

Antique shop: vintage, antique and contemporary jewellery, furniture, lighting, accessories, decorative objects, books

A shop specializing in vintage costume jewellery and accessories: Trifari, Coro Craft, Schiaparelli, Miriam Haskell, Har, Chanel, Boucher, Hobe, Joseff of Hollywood, Regency, Weiss, Christian Dior, Roger Jean-Pierre, Stanley Hagler, Schreiner, and so on; from the 1920s to the 1960s. It also sells antique and contemporary jewellery, as well as offering a range of antique and decorative objects, furniture and lighting.

Timothy Mark

20 New Quebec Street, W1 ＊ 020 7616 9390 ＊ www.timothymark.co.uk ＊ Tube: Marble Arch; Bus: 6, 23, 94, 274 ＊ Mon–Fri 12:00 — 17:00, Sat by appointment

Future antique shop: hand-crafted furniture and accessories

A new furniture and accessories designer of taste and innovation, Mr Mark produces hand-crafted, original furniture in a style all his own. True, it owes a good deal to classic designs, yet his approach and unusual touches make it recognizably different. If you are looking for future antiques, this small shop is the place for chairs, tables, sideboards, bedheads, clocks and wardrobes, all well-designed, one-off pieces. Unusual veneers and native woods are used sometimes as embellishments.

Andrew Nebbett Antiques

35-37 Church Street, NW8 * **020 723 2303** *
www.andrewnebbett.com * **Tube: Marylebone; Bus: 6, 23, 27,
453** * **Tues–Sat 10:00 – 17:30**

Antique shop: antiques from 1750–1950 from the UK and Scandinavia

Owner Andrew Nebbett travels throughout the UK and Scandinavia to choose his superb stock. Wares within the spacious, two-floor shop include painted and mahogany furniture, mirrors, lamps, industrial and garden furniture, and assorted decorative objects. Some unusual items are thrown into the mix as well; at the time of writing the shop was selling leather gym mats from 1930s Germany as floor coverings in a lovely, buttery brown.

While you're in the area...
THE WALLACE COLLECTION

Hertford House, Manchester Square, W1 * **020 7563 9500**
* **www.wallacecollection.org** * **Tube: Bond Street; Bus: 6,
23, 94, 139, 189** * **Daily 10:00 – 17:00** * **Free admission**

A superlative and varied picture and antiques collection in a fine 19th-century mansion. The collection consists of splendid furniture and pictures, chainmail and armour, including some exotic pieces, and numerous weapons. There is also lots of vases, porcelain, platters, urns and boxes, as well as small objets d'art and busts of French notables.

Stoke Newington

The name Stoke Newington means 'new town in a wood', and much of it was built in the mid-19th century. Although quite far from the centre of London, Stoke Newington is very much an urban village, and has been popular with a tribe of artists and writers for some time. In fact, it it is the birthplace of Daniel Defoe, and Edgar Allan Poe lived here later on. The area surrounds what was once the Roman Ermine Street (now the A10), marking the present High Street.

The Cobbled Yard

1 Bouverie Road, N16 * 020 8809 5286 * www.cobbled-yard.co.uk * Mainline station: Stoke Newington; Bus: 67, 73, 149 * Wed–Sun 11:00—17:30

Shop: early 20th-century furniture, decorative accessories, general bric-à-brac

The early 20th century is the source of many of the interesting items on show here. There is a large stock of reasonably priced pine furniture and also decorative accessories for sale, as well as some solid Edwardian pieces. The array of general and decorative items, which includes everything from brass and iron beds to accessories and pots, extends to specialist items and general bric-à-brac. A valuations service is offered, and furniture restoration and upholstery work is undertaken.

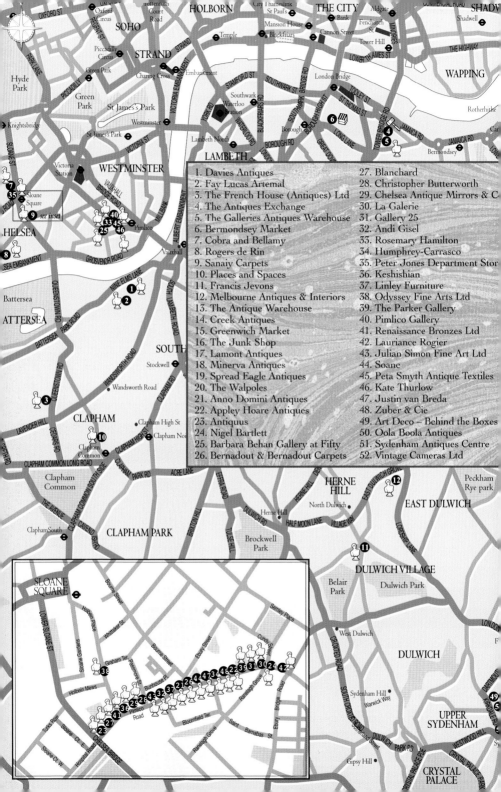

1. Davies Antiques
2. Fay Lucas Artemal
3. The French House (Antiques) Ltd
4. The Antiques Exchange
5. The Galleries Antiques Warehouse
6. Bermondsey Market
7. Cobra and Bellamy
8. Rogers de Rin
9. Sanaiy Carpets
10. Places and Spaces
11. Francis Jevons
12. Melbourne Antiques & Interiors
13. The Antique Warehouse
14. Creek Antiques
15. Greenwich Market
16. The Junk Shop
17. Lamont Antiques
18. Minerva Antiques
19. Spread Eagle Antiques
20. The Walpoles
21. Anno Domini Antiques
22. Appley Hoare Antiques
23. Antiquus
24. Nigel Bartlett
25. Barbara Behan Gallery at Fifty
26. Bernadout & Bernadout Carpets

27. Blanchard
28. Christopher Butterworth
29. Chelsea Antique Mirrors & C
30. La Galerie
31. Gallery 25
32. Andi Gisel
33. Rosemary Hamilton
34. Humphrey-Carrasco
35. Peter Jones Department Stor
36. Keshishian
37. Linley Furniture
38. Odyssey Fine Arts Ltd
39. The Parker Gallery
40. Pimlico Gallery
41. Renaissance Bronzes Ltd
42. Lauriance Rogier
43. Julian Simon Fine Art Ltd
44. Soane
45. Peta Smyth Antique Textiles
46. Kate Thurlow
47. Justin van Breda
48. Zuber & Cie
49. Art Deco – Behind the Boxes
50. Oola Boola Antiques
51. Sydenham Antiques Centre
52. Vintage Cameras Ltd

South London

Parts of South London are more prolific in antiques than others. While Battersea, Bermondsey and Sydenham have modest offerings, Pimlico has an embarrassment of riches. Greenwich has some interesting shops too, as well as some famous palaces, including the lovely Queen's House, by architect Inigo Jones. In Greenwich Park is the old Royal Observatory, which stands on the 0° line of longitude. The Maritime Museum was recently renovated, and its spacious rooms re-launched. Also worth a visit is the handsome Dulwich Picture Gallery, with its formidable collection of paintings by Eastern European Old Masters.

Battersea

Battersea lies on the south bank of the River Thames, just across from Chelsea, via the beautifully illuminated 19th-century Albert Bridge. Once largely industrial, the area is now very residential, with overspill coming in from fashionable Chelsea across the river. Battersea Park, once a popular spot for duelling, is now home to a zoo and the London Peace Pagoda. Another landmark is the Battersea Power Station, the first coal-fired electricity generator in the National Grid power distribution system. Now a Grade II listed building, it is slated to become a commercial and entertainment complex.

Davies Antiques

c/o The Packing Shop, 6-12 Ponton Road, SW8 *
020 8947 1002 * www.antique-meissen.com *
Tube: Vauxhall; Bus: 2, 36, 77 * Mon–Fri 09:30 – 17:30

Antique showroom: fine porcelain

After over 25 years of specializing in Meissen porcelain from the early 18th and 19th centuries, as well as the Art Nouveau and Art Déco periods, Hugh Davies has closed his Kensington Church Street gallery and now sells to collectors and dealers by appointment from this new location. His stock can be viewed during the hours listed above.

Fay Lucas Artmetal

Christie's Fine Art Security, 42 Ponton Road, SW8 * 020 7371 4404 * e-mail: info@faylucas.com * Tube: Vauxhall; Bus: 2, 36, 77 * By appointment only

Storehouse & salesrooms: mostly 20th-century furniture, jewellery, military and sporting items

The famed auctioneers Christie's has a vast brick-built storehouse here, in the shadow of the main railway line, and this place is under its wing. Furniture (mostly 20th century), good silverware, antique jewellery, military and sporting items, as well as gems are on offer here. Many articles are signed. Services include restoration and valuations.

The French House (Antiques) Ltd

125 Queenstown Road, SW8 * **020 7978 2228** * **www.thefrenchhouse.co.uk** * **Mainline rail: Queenstown Road; Bus: 137, 156** * **Mon–Sat 10:00 – 18:00**

Antique shop: French 18th- and 19th-century furniture

This pleasant shop has been on the busy Queenstown Road for over ten years. The couple running it have only French articles for sale,

Vintage antique jewellery at Fay Lucas.

from chests and wooden beds of the 18th and 19th centuries, to handsome 19th-century mirrors. Monthly buying trips allow for individual pieces to be sourced for customers.

Services

W. J. Cook Antique Restorations
167 Battersea High Street, SW11 * **020 7736 5329** * **www.antiquerestoration.uk.com** * **Mainline rail: Clapham Junction; Bus: 35, 39, 219** * **By appointment only**

A member of the British Antique Furniture Restorers Association, this workshop specializes in hand-carving, cabinet-making, gilding, French polishing, lock repairs, replacement leather, reupholstery and removal of water marks. Their in-house library is used to verify historical accuracy, and original 18th- and 19th-century tools are often employed to make the repairs.

Bermondsey

This is the first suburb you come to if you cross London Bridge and turn left along Tooley Street: it is an old-style working-class area with low-rise apartment buildings set amongst railway lines, arched embankments and creeks. The area off Tower Bridge has recently become a smart dormitory for City types, and a range of new flats borders, and sometimes overlooks, the River Thames. Bermondsey has some bargain places to shop and, most importantly, it is the home of the weekly Bermondsey Market.

The Antiques Exchange

170-172 Tower Bridge Road, SE1 * 020 7403 5568 * www.antiquesexchange.com * Tube: London Bridge; Bus: 53, 453 * Auctions held at 14:00 on the first Sunday of every month

Auction house: antique and reproduction furniture and objects

This auction house buys and sells a large selection of antiques, from silver and gold to glass and china objects. They also sell tables, chairs, desks, wardrobes and lamps.

The Galleries Antiques Warehouse

157 Tower Bridge Road, SE1 * 020 7407 5371 * Tube: London Bridge; Bus: 53, 453 * Mon–Thurs 09:30—17:30, Sat & Sun 12:00—18:00

Large shop: antique bookcases, desks and bedroom furniture

This cavernous warehouse offers a wide array of antiques, from the 1700s all the way to the 1950s. A good selection of bookcases, desks and bedroom furniture.

Bermondsey Market

Bermondsey Square, corner of Long Lane and Bermondsey Street, E1 * 020 7277 4597 * Tube: Borough; Bus: 53, 453 * Fri only 04:00—15:00, shops start closing at 12:00

Early birds get the best deals at the Bermondsey Market.

Business here begins very early. The public, usually die-hard antiques hunters, comes at any time, and flashlights and magnifying glasses are brandished as newly arrived stock is assessed: much of the stuff quickly changes hands, usually to other dealers. A good friend has been selling here and at Covent Garden for many years, and she still finds both locations good for business, even if Bermondsey has fewer stalls than it once did. Buy from reputable stalls if you can, as there are stories circulating about Bermondsey being a place to unload stolen goods. You'll find all sorts of stuff for sale here, from jewellery to junk, cutlery to curios, porcelain to pottery.

Some stalls at Bermondsey specialize, while others offer mixed goods.

While you're in the area...

THE DESIGN MUSEUM

Shad Thames, Butler's Wharf, SE1 * 0870 833 9955 * www.designmuseum.org * Tube: Tower Hill; Bus: 15, 78, 100 * Daily 10:00 – 17:45, last admission 17:15 * Admission fee

Take the first stairs down to the left from Tower Bridge and walk along the river path. This riverside museum is a repository of new and upcoming design, though it also shows classics from the 20th century.

THE HORNIMAN MUSEUM

100 London Road, Forest Hill * www.horniman.ac.uk Tube: Forest Hill; Bus: 176, 185, 312, P4 * Daily 10:30 – 17:30 * Free admission

A mixed collection holding in total some 350,000 objects and related items. There are three main collections here: World Cultures (Ethnography), Natural History (over 250,000 specimens) and Musical Instruments (over 7,000 instruments). There are other collections as well in this handsome museum, with its terraced gardens affording a splendid view of London.

THE TATE MODERN

Bankside, SE1 * 020 7887 8000 * www.tate.org.uk * Tube: Southwark; Bus: RV1, 45, 63, 100, 381 * Sun–Thurs 10:00 – 18:00, Fri & Sat 10:00 – 22:00 * Free admission

A new landmark, the old riverside power station was restored in 2000 as a grand museum of modern works; now its one-time chimney is a beacon of art. The Tate Modern displays the national collection of modern and contemporary art (art created since 1900) from all of the major movements, from Fauvism to Pop, and from Abstract Expressionism to Minimalist. All major artists are represented.

Chelsea

The King's Road and the Fulham Road, extending west from Chelsea to Knightsbridge, offer worthwhile walks amongst concentrations of high-quality shops. Newly developed from the ground around the old Duke of York's barracks is another smart shopping precinct: the Duke of York Square. The Square is also the site of an annual antique show hosted by the British Antiques Dealers Association (BADA).

Cobra and Bellamy

149 Sloane Street, SW1 * 020 7730 9993 * e-mail: www.cobrabellamy.co.uk * Tube: Sloane Square; Bus: 19, 22, 137 * Mon–Sat 10:30 – 17:30

Small shop: jewellery

Messrs Manussis and Hunter manage this trim, small shop not far from Knightsbridge. The stock is comprised of very smart and well chosen jewellery. Some of the jewellery is modern, yet there is an accent on the 20th century, all the way back to Edwardian gems in period settings. Art Déco pieces are also prominent.

Rogers de Rin

76 Royal Hospital Road, SW3 * 020 7352 9007 * Tube: Sloane Square; Bus: 11, 137, 239 * Mon-Fri 10:00 – 17:30, Sat 10:00 – 13:00

*A **collector's shop:** pottery animals, woolwork pictures, valentines*

Pimlico Road becomes the Royal Hospital Road as it passes the 17th-century Chelsea Hospital, home of the red-coated pensioners. At the junction with the narrow Paradise Walk, this charming little shop has been here for over 35 years. It is replete with lots of surprises – for example, Victoria de Rin is a dealer in pottery animals – and there are lots of them, especially the painted porkers of the Wemyss Family of Pigs! There is some furniture here too, along with woolwork pictures, tortoiseshell items and 'sailor' valentines. 'It's a collector's shop', Mrs de Rin explains.

Sanaiy Carpets

57 Pimlico Road, SW1 * 020 7730 4742 *
www.sanaiycarpets.co.uk * Tube: Sloane Square; Bus: 11, 211,
239 * Mon–Sat 10:00 – 17:30, or by appointment

Shop: *Oriental and Persian carpets, European and exotic tapestries, carpet
cushions*

A very eye-catching show window indeed here, and usually with one well-
illuminated antique carpet on display. Within, there is a good range of fine antique
Oriental and Persian carpets and small rugs, all carefully stored. There are tapestries
too, both European and exotic, as well as carpet cushions. Owner Hassan Sanaiy
expresses his love for beautiful rugs in his wares, and can talk about them
knowledgeably.

Antique Persian, Anatolian and Asian carpets at Sanaiy Carpets.

Clapham

Situated on the south bank of the River Thames, this is one of London's more spacious 'villages', with a 220-acre common surrounded by tall old houses and villas of considerable architectural and historic style, often with gardens. This is a popular residential area, particularly for young professionals with children. The area around Old Town, the High Street and Abbeville Road is full of shops, bars and restaurants, and the village atmosphere makes for a lively stroll.

Places and Spaces

30 Old Town, SW4 * 020 7498 0998 *
www.placesandspaces.com * Tube: Clapham Common; Bus: 35, 37, 155 * Mon–Sat 10:30 – 18:00, Sun 12:00 – 16:00

Small shop: 20th-century arts; contemporary and vintage furniture, lighting

This small and welcoming shop has been here for over 10 years and is dedicated to the 20th-century arts, and not just Art Déco. An eclectic mix of interior products from established designers is on offer here, along with those that are up-and-coming. Contemporary and vintage furniture, lighting and accessories are available. Owner Laura Slack not only offers valuations, but will also source vintage classics or their modern reproductions.

Dulwich

A delightful, attractive suburb on the way down to Greenwich, there is plenty of space and open air in Dulwich. Controls on development have allowed the area to survive as one of the few remaining 'villages' in London, and an overall rural feeling still pervades; indeed, the last farm closed down only in the 20th century. Alongside Dulwich's parks, lines of handsome small villas border its leafy, affluent streets. The Dulwich Picture Gallery is one of the area's great treasures, with its collection of Eastern European Old Master paintings.

Francis Jevons

80 Dulwich Village, SE21　*　020 8693 1991　*　Tube: North Dulwich station; Bus: 37, P4　*　Mon–Fri 09:30–13:00, 14:30–17:30; Sat 09:30–17:00, or by appointment

Antique shop: 18th- and 19th-century furniture, porcelain, lamps

Off College Road, this long-established, attractive shop sells mostly smaller pieces of 18th- and 19th-century furniture, plus a wide range of decorative items of the period, including a good selection of porcelain and lamps. Speciality restoration and valuations are undertaken upon request; there is also an interior design service.

Melbourne Antiques & Interiors

8 Melbourne Grove, East Dulwich, SE22　*　020 8299 4257　*　www.melbourneantiques.co.uk　*　Mainline rail: East Dulwich; Bus: 37　*　Mon–Sat 10:00–18:00

Antique shop: unusual furniture of French origin

This large shop sells a wide range of unusual furniture. Most of the items for sale are of French origin, including large, practical pieces such as typical armoires and chests. There is painted furniture in the same distinctive Gallic style here, too, as well as beds, chairs, mirrors, side tables and commodes. There is also a furniture restoration service.

While you're in the area...
DULWICH PICTURE GALLERY

Gallery Road, SE21 * 020 8693 5254 * www.dulwichpicturegallery.org.uk * Mailine rail: West Dulwich; Bus: P4, P13 * Tues–Fri 10:00—17:00; Sat & Sun 11:00—17:00 * Admission fee

England's first public art gallery, this one-time royal collection was put together for the King of Poland at the end of the 18th century, but it never left these shores. London surely benefited from the king's loss, as here you'll find a whole horde of Eastern European Old Master paintings of the 1600s and 1700s, well placed in the spacious rooms of this handsome gallery. The collection is one of the oldest of its kind in Britain.

DULWICH COLLEGE

Dulwich Common, SE21 * 020 8693 3601 * www.dulwichorg.co.uk * Mailine rail: West Dulwich; Bus: 3, P4, P13

A scenic college with a rich history, this school was founded by Edward Alleyn in 1619, with a letter patent from King James I. Alleyn was an actor and an entrepreneur, a colourful and famous figure of the day. One famous alumnus of the college is writer P G Wodehouse, who named it 'Valley Fields' in his books and described his years here as 'six years of unbroken bliss'. Sir Ernest Shackleton, the great Antarctic explorer, is another well-known alumnus. Take a stroll around the idyllic campus and admire its buildings, most of which were designed and built by Charles Barry, Junior, the eldest son of Sir Charles Barry, the architect of London's Houses of Parliament. Barry was President of the Royal Institute of British Architects from 1876-79, and his award of their prestigious gold medal in 1877 cited the New College at Dulwich, along with his other famous work.

Greenwich

This is one of London's most intriguing boroughs, with fine buildings and many scientific and historic aspects, from the chaste white Queen's House built for the wife of James I, to the Royal Observatory, home of Greenwich Mean Time and the Prime Meridian Line. Here also are the Maritime Museum and the *Cutty Sark*, the last surviving tea-clipper. In a now-vanished palace in the vast spread of Greenwich Park, Henry VIII was born, as were his daughters, Mary and Elizabeth. The same park is the starting point of the London Marathon, which takes place every Spring.

The Antique Warehouse

9-14 Deptford Broadway, SE8 * 020 8691 3062 * www.antiquewarehouse.co.uk * Rail: Deptford, New Cross; Bus: 53, 177, 47 * Mon–Sat 10:00–18:00, Sun 11:00–16:00

Antique warehouse: good furniture from 1750 up to the early 20th century; lighting fixtures

In nearby Deptford, on the way to Greenwich from London, this is a rambling place that has been established for over 20 years, with a lot to browse through. There is a large stock of good furniture, from 1750 to the early 20th century, including chairs, mirrors, sofas, tables, chests and lighting fixtures. A valuation service is offered as well.

Creek Antiques

23 Greenwich South Street, SE10 * 020 8293 5721 * e-mail: creekantiques@aol.com * Mainline rail: Greenwich; Bus: 180, 199 * By appointment only

Small shop: general antiquities; silver and plate; oddities

This small outlet is located handily near the rail station. On sale here is a mixed bag of articles ranging from general antiquities to silver and plate, and oddities such as old enamel signs and even amusement machines.

Greenwich Market

Greenwich Church Street, SE10 * 020 8293 3110 *
www.greenwich-market.co.uk * Tube: Greenwich; Bus: 53,
53X, 180, 188 * Antique market: Sat & Sun 09:00–17:00

Market: mainly 20th-century collectables and bric-à-brac

Contained and almost concealed within a twin block of 19th-century buildings, this market is used as a regular local market during the week. With around 40 stands, it isn't big, but that alone is a good reason for coming to this riverside settlement with its own character. On sale here are mainly 20th-century collectables and bric-à-brac, including coins, banknotes, medals, second-hand books and Art Déco furniture.

Vintage accessories at Greenwich Market.

The Junk Shop

9 Greenwich South Street, SE10 *
020 8305 1666 *
www.spreadeagle.org *
Mainline station: Greenwich; Bus: 180, 199 * open every day 10:00–17:30

Antique shop: collection of 18th- and 19th-century furnishings

The name is a bit misleading, as this is not really a dusty dump of oddities or rubbish (although they do describe some stuff as bric-à-brac). This shop actually stocks some rather good articles, especially the impressive array of 18th- and 19th-century furnishings and interesting architectural pieces, all set out in these roomy and very central premises.

98

Decorative items up to the 1950s are also sold. Established over 20 years ago, the shop is located close to Greenwich Rail Station.

Lamont Antiques

Tunnel Avenue Antique Warehouse, Tunnel Avenue Trading Estate, SE10 * 020 8305 1805 * www.lamontantiques.com * Tube: North Greenwich; Bus: 108, 188, 422 * Mon–Sat 09:00 – 17:30

Antique warehouse: large architectural articles

Not easy to get to (on the loop road around the Thames crossing of the Blackwall Tunnel), but handy for designers on new projects, or buyers needing, for example, den bars. This is basically a resource for those seeking to re-mount objects for restaurants or hotels. Be prepared for large architectural articles, including pub mirrors and mahogany bars, fitments recovered from ships, all kinds of old signs and fittings and stained glass panels. Container packing service.

Minerva Antiques

90 Royal Hill, Greenwich, SE10 * 020 8691 2221 * www.minerva-antiques.co.uk * Mainline rail: Greenwich; Bus: 177, 180, 199 * Tues–Sun 10:00 – 18:00

Antique shop: 19th-century furniture, English and French mirrors

A pleasant shop on a road climbing the hill above Greenwich Park, with some fine old houses in the neighbourhood. A place for antique furniture, as Mr Atkins stocks good pieces from the 19th century. He specializes in mirrors, both English and French, often in gilded frames. He also offers repair services and restorations, including chair caning, gilding and upholstery.

Spread Eagle Antiques

1 Stockwell Street, SE10 * 020 8305 1666 * www.spreadeagle.org * Mainline rail: Greenwich; Bus: 180, 199 * open every day 10:00 – 17:30

Antique shop: 18th- and 19th-century furniture and pictures

Occupying a prominent corner site beside Greenwich's theatre, and marked with a gilded sign, this shop is crammed with 18th- and 19th-century furniture and pictures, along with decorative items from the 18th century onwards. Restorations and valuations on furniture and pictures are also offered. Nearby at 8 Nevada Street is the **Spread Eagle Book and Curio Shop**: it has same hours and contact details as above, and sells a stock of antiquarian books, prints, postcards, period costumes and general curios.

The Walpoles

18 Nelson Road, Greenwich, SE10 * **020 8305 3080** * **www.walpoleantiques.com** * **Tube: Island Gardens (DLR); Bus: 53, 54, 177, 180, 188** * **Tues–Sat 10:00 – 18:00, Sun & Mon by appointment**

Antique shop: navy and army items; also furniture, paintings

This atmospheric shop is situated in the centre of Greenwich, near the river and Greenwich Pier, not far from the rail station. Appropriate to this town, the specialities of Graham Walpole are navy and army items. These range from 1740–1940, including colonial aspects. There is also a range of furniture, paintings and works of art. Chinese exports are sold here as well. Rentals of stock to TV and film companies. Also at the Van Arcade, 107 Portobello Road, every Sunday.

While you're in the area...
RANGER'S HOUSE

Greenwich Park, SE10 * **0870 333 181** * **Mailine rail: Greenwich; Bus: 53, 54, 177, 180, 188** * **Open Mar–Sept Wed–Sun 10:00 – 17:00** * **Admission fee**

A fabulous collection of gems, medieval ivories, pictures, porcelains and decorative arts of the Renaissance fills twelve of the rooms of this handsome house on the edge of Blackheath and Greenwich Park, originally built in 1699. A considerable attraction of the collection on show is the Renaissance jewels, most of them enamelled and brilliantly gemmed. Some of the house's original early 17th- century portraits are also still here.

TPR · F · HENGER,
Nº1·TROOP·Q·O·Y·D·
DONCASTER.

The Walpoles is a treasure trove for naval and military enthusiasts.

Pimlico

This fascinating area of early 19th-century houses with pale, stuccoed terraces is concentrated near Victoria Station. The area is largely residential, with many small hotels here as well. The Pimlico Road itself extends along from the Buckingham Palace Road across and beyond the Chelsea Bridge Road to the Royal Hospital buildings. If you want to take an easy stroll alongside a closely packed number of high-quality shops, try this road. Moreton Street is also noteworthy as an up-and-coming shopping destination. As well, there are several interesting charity and used-clothing shops in the area that are worth a trawl.

Anno Domini Antiques

66 Pimlico Road, SW1 * 020 77305496 * Tube: Sloane Square; Bus: 11, 211, 239 * Mon–Fri 12:15–17:30, Sat 10:00–15:00

Antique shop: 17th- and 18th-century furniture, glassware

This is a delightful shop with an old-style atmosphere and a history – at 30 years old it is claimed to be the first shop to have arrived on the Pimlico Road. On two levels, most of the period furniture here (chests, chairs, mirrors) is from the 17th and 18th centuries. Decanters and Georgian glass are also specialties, and so are various decorative items, including celery and bulb vases.

Appley Hoare Antiques

30 Pimlico Road, SW1 * 020 7730 7070 * www.appleyhoare.com * Tube: Sloane Square; Bus: 11, 211, 239 * Mon–Fri 10:00–18:00, Sat 10:00–16:00

Antique and flower shop: stone and metal garden ornaments, clay pots

Partly a flower shop to one side, it's not surprising that antique stone and metal garden ornaments should figure prominently here. Lots of clay pots, too, in classic and unusual shapes. An eclectic mixture of grotesque and often weathered urns, as well as frogs, dogs, pelicans and storks, spills out on to the wooden floors of the large room in profusion, mingling with venerable French country antiques, benches and plate racks, many primitive in style. You can find huge armoires here, too.

Antiquus

90–92 Pimlico Road, SW1 * 020 7730 8681 * www.antiquus-london.co.uk * Tube: Sloane Square; Bus: 11, 211, 239 * Mon–Sat 09:30–17:30

Antique shop: furniture, mirrors, lamps, bibelots

This small and secretive double-windowed shop looks like a

A splendid mix of garden items and French country furniture is sold at Appley Hoare.

stage as it reveals a dramatically lit, theatrical interior. The cleverly designed windows frame a sort of treasure chest, opened up with flickering 'candle flames' and other hidden lights glancing off on to mostly Gothic and Renaissance polished furniture, old gilt-framed mirrors, candlesticks, lamps and brackets as well as a clutter of intriguing and unusual bibelots. Corals are another interest, with plenty on offer.

Nigel Bartlett

22 Pimlico Road, SW1 * 020 7730 3223 * Tube: Sloane Square; Bus: 11, 211, 239 * Mon–Fri 10:00–17:00, appointment advisable

Gallery: butlers' trays and metal umbrella stands, marble mantelpieces, unusual sculpture, vases, glass and metal chandeliers

103

Grandiose, looming chimney-pieces and accessories fill the large, white-framed windows, and rest upon the smart black marble floors of this airy gallery. In the showroom, a range of odd articles jostles for attention. The owners like an eclectic style, and so you get mixes of different items, from butlers' trays and metal umbrella stands to marble mantelpieces and unusual pieces of sculpture. Vases, urns, bibelots and other works of art abound. A great and varied range of glass and metal chandeliers of many styles and periods hangs overhead.

Barbara Behan Gallery at Fifty

50 Moreton Street, SW1 * **0207 821 8793** * **www.barbarabehan.com** * **Tube: Pimlico; Bus: 24, 360** * **Tues–Sat 11:00 – 18:00, or by appointment**

Contemporary gallery: *modern arts*

New to the area, this elegant little gallery is indicated with a pavement feature: a sculpted tree stump in metal stands outside its pretty lime-flower green exterior. Walk through the door to find that inside it's an airy, white-walled gallery with a stylish wooden 'flagged' floor. A circular stair leads to a lower room. Regular exhibitions and special shows are presented here, mostly contemporary, but there may well be art from other centuries among the scheduled shows.

Bernardout and Bernardout Carpets

52 Pimlico Road, SWI * **020 7259 9090** * **Tube: Sloane Square; Bus: 24, 360** * **Mon–Fri 10:30 – 5:30, Sat by appointment**

Shop: *antique wall hangings, carpets, tapestry-covered cushions, rugs, cleaning and restoration*

Fine antique hangings swathe the walls, together with a range of carpets, all beautifully and dramatically lit; these are the lure here. This is no ordinary carpet shop, and a good deal of stylish invention has gone into displaying the high quality stock. The large show window reveals great piles of tapestry-covered cushions, scattered before an antique hanging, and beyond, a series of sumptuous rugs are laid out, their gorgeous, soft colouring beautifully contrasted with the grey-blue floor. There is also a special interest in Aubusson carpets, which can be cleaned and restored here.

Blanchard

86-88 Pimlico Road, SW1 * **020 7823 6310** * **Tube: Pimlico;
Bus: 24, 360** * **Mon–Fri 10:00 – 18:00, Sat by appointment**

*Antique shop: 17th- and 18th-century French pieces, pictures, garden
furniture, bronzes*

Full of delightful contrasts, this is a most charming and welcoming two-level shop.
The accent is on fine French pieces here. Standing on bare wooden floors among the
grand 17th- and 18th-century cabinets and fine mirrors are big wooden tubs and
grandiose stone urns, lamps and several busts. There are many oddities, too, from
inlaid tables to wooden cross-cut panels in unusual woods. Pictures and prints are on
offer as well, along with a collection of charming bronzes.

Christopher Butterworth

71 Pimlico Road, SW1 * **020 7823 4554** *
e-mail: crb@christopherbutterworth.com * **Tube: Pimlico;
Bus: 24, 360** * **Mon–Fri 09:00 – 18:00, Sat by appointment**

Antique shop: lighting, icons, period furniture, busts, sconces

There is a mixed lot of dramatic stuff here, and most prominent are the huge lamps
and other period lighting fixtures; note also the impressive range of icons that glows
in the window. In this intriguing shop there are also some fine examples of elegant
period furniture from France, England and Italy peeping out and almost hidden
under a welter of smaller antique items. Lots of classic busts are on show as well,
along with some grandiose wall sconces.

Chelsea Antique Mirrors & Co.

72 Pimlico Road, SW1 * **0920 7824 8024** * **Tube: Pimlico;
Bus: 24, 360** * **Mon–Fri 09:00 – 18:00; Sat 10:00 – 14:00**

Gallery: English, French and Italian mirrors in many sizes and ages

Somehow it seems that Chelsea shops have an accent on splendid mirrors, and if you
enjoy these glittering pieces of truly elegant period furniture, then for you, Andrew
Kolbuszowski's gallery is an ideal place. Once beyond the shop's small, grey-green
front, the mirrors show up particularly well on the interior deep green walls

complemented by dark carpets. There are English, French and Italian mirrors in all sizes, with some fine gilded and convex examples. Periods range from the 16th to the 19th centuries. The firm is also a specialist place for gilding and carving.

La Galerie

24 Pimlico Road, SW1 ＊ 020 7730 3111 ＊ Tube: Pimlico; Bus: 24, 360 ＊ Mon–Sat 10:00 – 18:00

Gallery: 19th- and 20th-century pictures, 19th-century Russian furniture

This is a really charming gallery with unusual exhibitions – when I visited, it was hosting a show featuring cartoons and portraits of animals in costume, several of them old. Pictures from the 19th and 20th centuries are favoured here, but this light and open space also has furniture – again, at the time of writing, some superb Russian pieces. Reminiscent of Biedermeier furniture, these highly polished chairs, sofas and tables are in seductive early 19th-century styles. Some of the pieces have unusual, rare wood veneers, often in glossy, exotic colorings.

Gallery 25

26 Pimlico Road, SW1 ＊ 020 7730 7516 ＊ Tube: Pimlico; Bus: 24, 360 ＊ Mon–Fri 09:00 – 18:00, Sat 10:00 – 14:00

Gallery: chandeliers in glass and metal; late 19th-century French and Art Déco furniture

A brilliant array of unusual and sometimes weird articles crams this high-ceilinged and well-lit gallery. Among the jumble of items, French owner David Iglesis sells chandeliers in glass and metal in a host of varied styles. If you are looking for a special one, there are lots of ornate examples of different periods, most displayed hanging from the high ceiling. Some of the furniture here is late 19th-century French, but there's quite a bit of interesting stock for the Art Déco fancier, too.

Andi Gisel

69 Pimlico Road, SW1 ＊ 020 7730 4187 ＊ e-mail: andigiselantique@aol.com ＊ Tube: Pimlico; Bus: 11, 24, 360 ＊ Mon–Fri 10:00 – 18:00, Sat 11:00 – 17:00

Antique shop: French garden sculptures, lighting fixtures and furniture, miscellaneous

An intimate shop crowded with all kinds of intriguing pieces, large and small. There's a lot to inspect here, and a charming flair for presentation: bowls of fruit and open books adorn the tables. Most items are French, with a charming country flavour, as evidenced by large stone flower and fruit garden sculptures. There is also an array of lighting fixtures (including outdoor ones) and furniture, from ancient armoires to chairs. Miscellaneous decorative items, such as drums, tapestries, bookshelves and candlesticks, often in fantastic styles, are also for sale.

Rosemary Hamilton

44 Moreton Street, SW1 * **020 7828 5018** * **Tube: Pimlico; Bus: 24, 360** * **Mon–Fri 09:30 – 17:30**

Modern shop: decorative items, including chandeliers, tassels, candlesticks

Behind the chaste white façade under its sunblind, this shop contains a collection of intriguing decorative items and a few actual antiques. Rosemary Hamilton is an interior design consultant, but she does have a good eye for the odd and eccentric, so several of the items on display in this attractive wood-floored shop may well catch your eye. Sale items include chandeliers, tassels, Art Déco-style mirrors, animal figures, some bizarre candlesticks, and dried flower arrangements in unusual containers.

Humphrey-Carrasco

43 Pimlico Road, SW1 * **020 7730 9911** * **Tube: Pimlico; Bus: 11, 24, 360** * **Mon–Fri 10:00 – 18:00**

Shop: Sculptures, late 18th- to early 19th-century furniture and lighting fixtures

Wrought ironwork decorates the 19th-century grey brick front of this elegant shop, making it stand out. Inside, its plain and severe wooden floor and the plain-painted walls of the showroom lend a strong feeling of period. This makes a fine backing for the well-chosen stock of sculptures and late 18th- to early 19th-century furniture. The furniture is shown together with some intriguing lamps and lighting fixtures of the same period, ranging from classic chandeliers to torchères and candlesticks.

Peter Jones Department Store

On the north-west corner of Sloane Square, SW1 * **020 7730 3434** * **Tube: Sloane Square; Bus: 11, 22, 137, 360** * **Mon–Sat 09:30 – 19:00, Sun 11.00 – 17:00**

Multiple store, antiques section: household pieces

This classic, fashionable store (part of the John Lewis partnership) is one of the increasingly rare multiple shops with a section devoted to a range of antiques. The shop is glamorous in an old-fashioned way, yet also stylish – a wide, deep well opens up the centre of the store, all white panels and glass, giving views into the departments, until you reach the 5th floor. Here, a spacious area houses a selection of good-quality antique pieces including, on a recent visit, gilded mirrors, Georgian chairs and tables, clocks, carpets and chests, mostly English 18th and 19th century.

Keshishian

73 Pimlico Road, SW1 * **020 7730 8810** * **www.keshishiancarpets.com** * **Tube: Pimlico; Bus: 24, 360** * **Mon–Fri 09:30 – 18:00, Sat 10:00 – 17:00**

Gallery: antique carpets and tapestries

Mostly European antique carpets, tapestries and Aubussons are the special attractions at this intimate corner gallery; you actually walk on the stock as a carpet is unrolled across the wooden floor at the entry. It also has an unusual speciality in Arts and Crafts and Art Déco carpets. The large window always features a well-illuminated tapestry or carpet, so it catches the eye and is easily spotted from the street. A cleaning and restoration service is available.

Linley Furniture

60 Pimlico Road, SW1 * **020 7730 7300** * **www.davidlinley.com** * **Tube: Pimlico; Bus: 11, 24, 360** * **Mon–Thurs 10:00 – 18:00, Fri–Sat 10:00 – 17:00**

Future antique shop: furnishings, glassware, hangings, carpets

A handsome, airy shop with a real sense of luxury on several levels that stretches to the street behind. There are mostly modern pieces here, but these are very stylish and are definitely in the category of 'antiques of the future'. Colours are strong and vibrant, with background panels of bottle greens and deep blues. There is lots to admire here, from a large range of furnishings and glassware, cutlery, lots of seating, sets of dining chairs and elegant low tables. The 'designer objects' here range from bibelots to geometric lamps and boxes in rare woods. Striking hangings, floor carpets, well chosen big pictures and framed photographs are also on offer.

Odyssey Fine Arts Ltd

24 Holbein Place, SW1 * **020 7730 9942** * **Tube: Sloane Square; Bus: 11, 211, 239** * **Mon–Fri 10:30 – 17:30, Sat 10:30 – 15:30**

Antique shop: porcelains, prints, crystals, Art Déco articles, 1960s items

Just off the Pimlico Road is this small, crowded shop with its handsome tiled floors. It contains many fascinating, if often eccentric, items – for example, the ornately depicted scene in jasper with *pietra dura* on their card is from an 18th-century Venetian console table. You'll find many Art Déco articles, 1960s stuff, and large crystals here, as well as porcelains and prints. There are several sets of prints usually displayed in collections on the walls: these are of the 18th and 19th centuries, and are for sale in their handsome frames.

The Parker Gallery

28 Pimlico Road, SW1 * **020 7730 6768** * **www.theparkergallery.com** * **Tube: Sloane Square; Bus: 11, 211, 239** * **Mon–Fri 09:30–17:30, Sat by appointment**

Gallery: picture and print dealers of marine and military sporting works, small antique items

An older and very atmospheric gallery: in fact, it was founded in 1750, and claims to be 'the oldest established firm of picture and print dealers'. There is a selection of items and unusual curios on view in the wide, well-lit windows, for this is not merely a picture gallery – there are lots of small antique items on sale, too. Allow plenty of time for a fascinating visit, for their large collection offers a huge stock of prints and pictures specializing in marine and military sporting works. The staff is always helpful.

Pimlico Gallery

39 Moreton Street, SW1 * **020 7976 6200** * **Tube: Victoria;**
Bus: 24, 360 * **Mon–Fri 10:00–17:30, Sat 10:00–14:00**

Gallery: prints and reproductions from the 16th to the 19th centuries

This is a charming, well-lit print gallery carpeted with Oriental rugs, its walls covered with many prints and reproductions, often in sequences and sets. Handsomely framed, the special pleasures here are cityscapes, floral and botanical subjects, even an array of brightly tinted and exotically costumed Ottoman sultans. Proprietor Walter Richards is welcoming, and has been at this location for some time; his stock covers a range of periods from the 16th to the 19th centuries.

Renaissance Bronzes Ltd

77 Pimlico Rd, SW1 * **020 7730 3005** *
www.renaissancebronzes.co.uk * **Tube: Sloane Square;**
Bus: 11, 24, 360 * **Mon–Fri 10:00–18:00**

Gallery: large sculptures, many in bronze, mostly from France

This is an airy, high-ceilinged gallery with a fine display of mostly large sculptures, many in bronze. The big animals, busts and statues can be viewed easily, as the pieces are well spaced and displayed against plain grey walls, backed with big house plants. The wares come mostly from France, but there are also some from England and Thailand.

Lauriance Rogier

20a Pimlico Road, SW1 * **020 7823 4780** * **Tube: Victoria;**
Bus: 11, 24, 360 * **Mon–Fri 10:00-18:00, Sat 11:00-16:00**

Corner shop: specialist items from all over France

Very French in flavour, this corner shop, with its pretty façade, is the place to look for a large array of lamps with often eccentric supports, such as wooden legs; otherwise there are many Gallic country antiques, and a charming collection of decided oddities culled from all over France. Probably bound for the specialist collector, or a decorator, the wares vary from cut-out wooden duck decoys to kitchen and farm implements. Also for sale are old books and a selection of ornaments.

Julian Simon Fine Art Ltd

70 Pimlico Road, SW1 * 020 7730 8673 *
www.19thcenturypaintings.com * Tube: Sloane Square;
Bus: 11, 24, 360 * Mon–Fri 10:00–18:00, Sat 10:00–16:00

Gallery: period pictures

A fine, wide gallery with well-hung and well-lit paintings. The works on show are almost all period pictures, and are of high quality; many are French, and most are of the 19th century. Some paintings depicting scenes from the countryside and various towns are of seriously good quality, while others are charmingly decorative.

Soane

50 Pimlico Road, SW1 * 020 7730 6400 * e-mail:
shop@soane.co.uk * Tube: Sloane Square; Bus: 11, 24, 360 *
Mon–Fri 09:30–18:00, Sat 10:30–16:30

Antique shop: pictures, furnishings, pottery, china, glassware

This is a small and neat little place, standing out in the street frontage with its style of a temple façade outlined in dark blue. Within, the shop is laid out to invite the eye by owner Lulu Lytle, and to charm with its well placed contents. Lots of pictures line the walls. With most pieces set under dramatic lighting, the shop has plenty to offer in both fine furnishings and antiques, though there are quite a few reproduction pieces. Pottery, china and glassware is also sold.

Peta Smyth Antique Textiles

42 Moreton Street, SWI * 020 7630 9898 * Tube: Victoria;
Bus: 24, 360 * Mon–Fri 09:30–17:30, closed Sat

Antique shop: antique hangings, panels, tapestries, needlework

Behind this unusual shop front you will find a special collection: crowded into the shop's atmospheric and theatrical interior is an eye-filling throng of picturesque antique hangings, panels and tapestries. Colours are rich and ravishing, and the selection ranges from large classic pieces of woven tapestry to embroidered chair seats. There are fabric scrolls, tapestry cushions and even the occasional costume. Needlework is a particular interest, with many fine examples, some to be seen in

111

panels framed for display. Otherwise, 'any furniture is here by accident', says the amiable owner.

Kate Thurlow

41 Moreton Street, SW11 ✻ 020 7738 0792 ✻ Tube: Victoria; Bus: 24, 360 ✻ Tues–Sat 10:00 – 18:00, otherwise by appointment

Specialist shop: 17th- and 18th-century Portuguese furniture, lighting fixtures

Another specialist place, and particularly fascinating, as this shop has a special focus: unusual furnishing and objects from Portugal. The unique chests, stools and chairs – often in walnut or beech wood – in this pleasing shop are mostly of the 17th and 18th centuries, with some from even earlier periods. There is an accent on mirrors and lighting fixtures too, some in rather bizarre designs. All of the wares here are all carefully selected by the very helpful Ms Thurlow.

Justin van Breda

45 Pimlico Road, SW1 ✻ 020 7730 3991 ✻ www.j-v-b.com ✻ Tube: Sloane Square; Bus: 11, 24, 360 ✻ Mon–Fri 10:00 – 18:00, Sat 10:00 – 17:00

Future antique shop: reproduction items constructed in South Africa

Two large metal vases mark the entry to this neat shop. There are no actual antiques exhibited here: almost every item a is high-quality reproduction. Pieces are beautifully made, finely finished, and all constructed in South Africa. These modern 'antiques' are mostly in Art Déco style, and many of the furnishings feature beautiful rare African woods and veneers, as well as the always fashionable mahogany, much to British taste, in deep brandy browns and dark reds. There are tables, stands, chairs, desks, chests and decorative articles, some Chinese in style.

Zuber & Cie.

42 Pimlico Road, SW1 ✻ 020 7824 8265 ✻ Tube: Sloane Square; Bus: 11, 24, 360 ✻ Mon–Fri 10:00 – 17:30

Shop: fine French wallpapers

This is an enchanting shop, selling only fine French wallpapers. The stock is extensive and is beautifully displayed. Almost everything is a careful reproduction of a historic design, crafted in the shop's 200-year-old factory in France. Wallpapers can feature up to 250 colours, yet a wall panel on sale here can cost as little as £150. There is a special training school (l'école Boulle) in the 12th district of Paris, where students work on these fantastically detailed wall coverings.

Services

Ebony and Co
198 Ebury St, SW1 * 020 7259 7755 * www.ebonyandco.com * Tube: Sloane Square; Bus: 11, 24, 360 * Mon–Fri 10:00 – 18:00, Sat by appointment

This large showroom is a place to buy simple wood choices for backgrounds. The shop provides flooring, panelling, even ceilings, in natural woods by the square metre. Most of these are new woods, and many are American and African (they don't use endangered tree species), but they can also locate antique woods for customers upon request.

Charity Shops in the Area

Amid this close-knit web of handsome early 19th-century terraces, house clearances can throw up real treasures, though good managers may well recognize them before you do. Around Tachbrook Street, Warwick Way, Ebury Street and Ebury Bridge Road are several worthwhile charity shops, from retro to rough. The newest shop to the area is called **KIDS** (40 Tachbrook St, 020 7630 7730). Selling mostly children's items, this shop also has a large range of vintage retro gear from the 1930s and the 1940s, from shoes and pillbox hats to furs and scarves. Yet another retro shop is **Cornucopia** (12 Upper Tachbrook St, 020 7828 5752), a place crowded with double racks offering clothes and accessories dating from 1910 to 1990. **The Trinity Hospice Charity Shop** (85 Wilton Road, 020 7931 7191) has some bargains; piled outside recently was a 1930s dining set. Best of all is a neat shop called the **Trinity Hospice** (Ebury Bridge Rd, 020 7787 1014). The helpful manageress runs a good shop, selling small, tasteful decorative items such as statues, clocks, vases and bric-à-brac. Sometimes she gets remarkable items, so much so that she maintains a contact at Christie's (see page 57), where they are valued and often accepted for sale, making good returns for her charity.

Sydenham

An interesting suburb towards the fringes of South East London, Sydenham is a leafy place, just beyond Dulwich and Forest Hill, with lots of open spaces and parks, and is well served by local rail lines. This was a place that impressed one of the Impressionist group: the painter Pisarro painted here. Along Kirkdale, the main street that bisects the districts of Upper and Lower Sydenham, there are several antique outlets, as well as a good vintage camera shop.

Art Déco – Behind the Boxes

98 Kirkdale, SE26 * 020 8291 6116 * www.behindtheboxes-artdeco.co.uk * British rail: Sydenham; Bus: 122, 176, 202, 312 * Tues–Sat 10:00 – 17:00, by appointment Sun & Mon

Antique shop: furniture of all sorts, lighting fixtures, costume jewellery from the 1930s

Mr Owen has been at this sizable place for almost 20 years, and is well established as a local dealer in furniture of all sorts. His speciality is Art Déco, and he has a range of lighting fixtures and costume jewellery: pieces are from the 1930s onwards. He offers valuations and shows periodically at Art Déco fairs.

Oola Boola Antiques

139-147 Kirkdale, SE26 * 020 8291 9999 * e-mail: oola.boola@telco4u.net * British rail: Sydenham; Bus: 122, 176, 202, 312 * Mon-Fri 10:00 – 18:00, Sat 10:00 – 17:00, Sun 11:00 – 17:00

Antique shop: retro, Victorian, Arts and Crafts, Art Déco and Art Nouveau furniture

An odd name indeed, yet worth a call, because here at these large premises behind a forecourt you'll find some unusual items. All sorts of retro stuff is for sale, plus a range of good furniture too, with lots of big Victorian and Arts and Crafts items priced from very low to high. For those who like the Art Déco and Art Nouveau styles, there are good possibilities, too. Shipping service.

Sydenham Antiques Centre

48 Sydenham Road, SE26 * 020 8778 1706 * British rail: Sydenham; Bus: 75, 122, 176, 194, 202 * Tues–Sat 10:30–17:30

Small shop: porcelain, china, glass, smaller furniture, jewellery

Mrs Cockburn has run her small shop at this location for over 10 years now. She offers plenty of porcelain, china and ornaments. Another aspect is a good deal of glass, as well as some smaller pieces of furniture and decorative items; jewellery and silver articles from the 19th century onwards are also available. As well, Mrs Cockburn offers valuations, and a restoration service for old china.

Vintage Cameras Ltd.

256 Kirkdale, SE26 * 0130 438 0218 * www.vintagecameras.co.uk * British rail: Sydenham; Bus: 122, 176, 202, 312 * Mon–Fri 10:00–17:00

Small shop: vintage and classic cameras

A vast selection of cameras, from the early brass and wood antiques of the early 19th century to the classic cameras of the 1930s, 1950s, 1960s and 1970s in a range of prices. Modern equipment is available as well, as are books, instruction manuals and other accessories. Valuations made. Mail order available.

Collectable cameras are sold alongside newer models at Vintage Cameras.

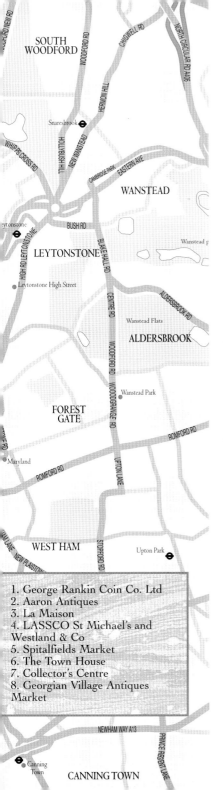

SOUTH
WOODFORD

Snaresbrook

WANSTEAD

LEYTONSTONE

Leytonstone High Street

Wanstead Flats

ALDERSBROOK

Wanstead Park

FOREST
GATE

Maryland

ROMFORD RD

WEST HAM

Upton Park

1. George Rankin Coin Co. Ltd
2. Aaron Antiques
3. La Maison
4. LASSCO St Michael's and
Westland & Co
5. Spitalfields Market
6. The Town House
7. Collector's Centre
8. Georgian Village Antiques
Market

NEWHAM WAY A13

Canning
Town

CANNING TOWN

East London

The East End of London is a
diverse and historically fascinating
region. Contained within its
boundaries are Tower Bridge and
the Tower of London, along with
more modern areas, such as
Canary Wharf and the Docklands.
'This most colourful corner of the
city', in the words of Charles
Dickens, who visited here as a
child – and later laboured here in
a factory – was the inspiration for
and the setting of many of
Dickens's novels. Other famous
past residents include Joseph
Stalin, and even Mahatma Ghandi
for a brief period. Today, the East
End remains as rich and eclectic
as ever, and is home to some
fascinating shops and markets.

Bethnal Green

Being in the shadow of The City, this area attracts large numbers of workers to its cheap restaurants and snack bars. Heading towards Bethnal Green, a sign indicates Petticoat Lane, once formidable, now essentially a fashion and fabric centre, as is the nearby market on Wentworth Street. This is the beginning of the East End, a distinctly poor neighbour-hood, with its Edwardian blocks and tight street layouts. There are plenty of shops, but alas, few selling antiques. The real treasure here is the Museum of Childhood: a must for any collector of children's items and a truly joyful experience.

George Rankin Coin Co. Ltd

325 Bethnal Green Road, E2 * 020 7729 1280 * Tube: Bethnal Green; Bus: 8, 388, D3 * Tues–Sat 09:00 – 17:30, or call ahead for an appointment

Antique shop: coins, medallions, decorations, jewellery

Established for over 40 years, and right on the main street, this old-fashioned shop is a local fixture. Not only does it have a large stock of antique coins, but it also sells a good selection of medallions and decorations. Some interesting jewellery here, too.

While you're in the area...
MUSEUM OF CHILDHOOD

Cambridge Heath, Bethnal Green, E2 * 020 8980 2415 * www.museumofchildhood.org.uk * Tube: Bethnal Green; Bus 8, 26, 48 * Sat–Thurs 10:00 – 17:30 * Free admission

This branch of the Victoria and Albert Museum is well worth seeking out. For those interested in antique children's toys, there are many fine examples, from 19th-century tin items to sophisticated mechanical animated models. There are wooden dolls, toy soldiers and teddy bears, with lots of early games, too.

Hackney

Just beyond Islington, along Essex Road, this one-time village gave London the term 'hackney carriage'. Today it is a lively place, with a mixed population from all over the world occupying a net of 19th-century streets. Mare Street, Hackney's main drag, is alive with people and lots of odd shops. Many of the shops are junky, but some sell fascinating curios, especially Caribbean, African, and increasingly, Turkish items, making for an interesting visit. Don't miss the Tudor Sutton house on Homerton High Street, with its fine period rooms and panelling.

Aaron Antiques

79 Pownall Road, E8 * **020 7249 1784** * **Tube: Bethnal Green; Bus: 236** * **Mon–Sat 09:00 – 5:30**

Depository of antiques: pre-war antiques; smaller items

Dalston adjoins Hackney to the west, and here, off the Queensbridge Road and close to the Regent's Canal, you will find this large depository of antiques. Aaron's functions largely as a buyer of all kinds of pre-war items, so it is a good location to know about for sales, clearances and valuations. They buy and stock a range of objects, from large pieces of furniture and paintings to smaller items such as jewellery and curios. Call before you visit.

While you're in the area... SUTTON HOUSE

2-4 Homerton High Street, E9 * **020 8986 2264** * **www.statelyhomes.com** * **Mainline rail: Homerton; Bus: 52, 394** * **Call for opening times** * **Admission fee**

This uniquely surviving house was built in 1535, when Hackney was still a village. Its original owner, Ralph Sadleir, was a rising star at the court of Henry VIII. Through the years it was home to successive merchants, Huguenot silk-weavers, Edwardian clergy and Victorian schoolmistresses. Its oak-panelled rooms and carved fireplaces have survived intact.

Shoreditch and Spitalfields

This essentially run-down area east of Liverpool Street Station, bordered by Hoxton, is blighted by rail lines, run-down housing and disused warehouses. In addition, Shoreditch High Street is a main road, busy with traffic: hardly a place one would expect to find an antique shop. However, there are a few very good specialist shops here, making it a worthwhile trip. Spitalfields, in particular, is home to the famous Spitalfields Market, which holds an antique market every Thursday. Extending north is Kingsland Road, home to the fascinating Geffrye Museum.

La Maison

107-108 Shoreditch High Street, E1 * **020 7729 9646** * **Tube: Shoreditch; Bus: 26, 35, 47, 48** * **Mon–Fri 10:00–18:00, Sat 11:30–18:00**

Large store: *French furniture and beds, restoration*

With the local history having a distinct French air – the weavers who settled in 17th-century Spitalfields were Huguenots escaping the persecutions of Louis XIV – it's interesting that this large store is French, owned by M and Mme Bacou, who are in attendance. Appropriately, this large shop features French stock, mostly furniture and beds. There is a restoration service, as well as a bespoke and a delivery service.

LASSCO St Michael's

St Michael's Church, Mark Street (off Paul Street), EC2 * **020 7749 9949. Other location: Brunswick House, 30 Wandsworth Road, SW8** * **www.lassco.co.uk** * **Tube: Old Street; Bus: 23, 214, 271** * **Mon–Fri 09:00-17:30, Sat 10:00-17:00**

Antique warehouse: *specializing in architectural antiques*

LASSCO (The London Architectural Salvage and Supply Co. Ltd) claims to be London's largest architectural antiques specialist. This enormous shop is crammed

Spectacular lighting and other architectural gems are found at LASSCO.

with marble mantles, stone chimneypieces, cast iron grates, columns, panelled rooms, decorative stonework, wrought iron gates, chandeliers, mirrors, stained glass, museum cabinets, church ornaments and brass hardware. Many of the specimens have been saved from some of Europe's most prestigious buildings, and then lovingly restored. Worth a visit whatever your budget.

Westland & Co.

Shares the St Michael's Church conversion with LASSCO (see above), EC2 * 020 7739 8094 * www.westland.co.uk * Tube: Old Street; Bus: 23, 214, 271 * Mon–Fri 09:00–18:00, Sat 10:00–17:00, Sun by appointment

Antique shop: specializing in period fireplaces, architectural elements and panelling

While you're in the area...
THE GEFFRYE MUSEUM

136 Kingsland Road, E2 * www.geffrye-museum.org.uk * Tube: Liverpool Street; Bus: 243 * Tues–Sat 10:00–17:00, Sun 12:00–17:00 * Free admission

This is a unique museum set in a terrace of 18th-century almshouses that were originally constructed for the Ironmongers' Company. Although this is very much a working district crowded with small houses and blocks of flats, the almshouses are set resplendently in wide gardens shaded by huge old trees. Inside, and demonstrating the changing styles of domestic interiors, are several rooms reflecting the changes of furnishings from the 17th century to the Georgian and Victorian periods onto the 1930s, ending appropriately with late 20th-century spaces in local warehouses. There are many good examples of period furniture and accoutrements here. Special exhibitions can feature an examination of various items of furniture, such as a detailed look at the development of the dining chair in England. An audio-guide tour is available, and as it is very much a 'local' museum, there are lots of activities and workshops.

Like LASSCO, this shop offers an extensive range of antique period and prestigious chimney-pieces and architectural elements. Styles range from Renaissance to Art Déco. They will arrange and advise on shipping, storage, insurance and installation.

Spitalfields Market

109 Commercial Street, Between Lamb and Brushfield Streets, E1 *
020 7247 6590 *
www.visitspitalfields.com
* **Tube: Liverpool Street; Bus: 8, 26, 35, 67**
* **General market: Mon–Fri 10:00 – 16:00; Antique market: Thurs 08:00 – 15:00; Organic food market: Sun 11:00 – 15:00**

Covered market: a wide variety of antiques and second-hand merchandise

From fashion to fishing tackle, Spitalfields Market has something to offer for just about everyone.

One of London's ongoing surprises – and a growing one, for Spitalfields Market is definitely improving week by week. Located opposite the great pile of the parish church of St George's, which dominates the small neighbourhood of 17th-century streets, the market has several entrances. Once inside the covered space you see a well-spaced parade of stalls spilling out. On Thursdays, these stalls are devoted to a wide variety of antiques and second-hand merchandise, including ceramics, vintage clothing and militaria.

The Town House

5 Fournier Street, E1 * 020 7247 4745 *
www.townhousewindow.co.uk * Tube: Aldgate East; Bus: 67 *
Thurs & Fri 11:30−18:00, Sat 10:30−17:00

Antique shop: 18th-century furniture, decorative: mirrors, paintings, glass

Standing beside the local church, this shop offers high-quality wares, mainly 18th-century English furniture and decorative items. The atmosphere both inside and outside of the shop is lovely, from the olive-brown street façade to the 'antique yellow' walls within. The shop's bare wooden floors, rugs, brick fireplaces and general décor all reflect what life might have been like 300 years ago in Spitalfields. The ground floor extends to a back window looking on to a tiny garden. Stock runs from ordinary to elegant mirrors, paintings, prints, busts, glass and candlesticks.

Georgian and Queen Anne furniture at the Town House in Spitalfields.

Walthamstow

A short distance to the north-east is the major suburb of Walthamstow. A pleasant place, with its green residential streets, there are great reservoirs to one side beyond Higham Hill, and stretches of parkland to the other. The centre clusters around the principal Forest Road. Famous residents include William Morris, one of the most influential designers of the Victorian age (local William Morris Gallery shows his work), and former British Prime Minister Benjamin Disraeli. There are two noteworthy antique centres in the area, both of which are well worth a visit.

Collector's Centre

98 Wood Street, E17 * 020 8520 4032 * Mainline rail: Wood Street; Bus: 230 * Mon–Sat 09:30 – 17:00, closed Thurs

Antique market: mainly 20th-century furniture from the 1950s–1960s

As it describes itself, this large, rambling market is indeed a collectors' place, but note the stock is mostly 20th-century furniture from the 1930s to the 1960s, from bargain prices up to quite high mark-ups for fashionable stuff. Also for sale are records, books and toys, as well as plenty of assorted small items.

Georgian Village Antiques Market

100 Wood Street, E17 * 020 8520 6638 * Mainline rail: Wood Street; Bus: 230 * Mon–Sat 10:00 – 17:00; closed Thurs

Antique market: prints to postcards, clocks, barometers, jewellery, precious metals

Established over 30 years ago, this is a neat centre for five antiques shops offering different antiques aspects. The range of goods runs from prints to stamps and postcards, and there are specialist places offering clocks and barometers. Brass and copper, as well as jewellery, silver and plate items are on sale as well.

1. Christine Bridge
2. Mary Cooke
3. The Dining Room Shop
4. Chiswick Fireplace Company
5. David Edmonds
6. Marshall Phillips
7. The Old Cinema
8. Oriental Furniture and Arts
9. Strand Antiques
10. Beaver Coin Room
11. Orsini Period Clothing
12. The Amphora
13. Birdie Fortescue
14. Decorative Antiques
15. Fulham Cross Antiques
16. The Furniture Shop
17. Lots Road Auctions
18. Lucy Johnson
19. Numbers 275, 291 & 313 Antiques
20. The Parson's Table
21. Stephen Long
22. Treasure Island
23. Architectural Antiques
24. Paravent
25. Rochtel Interiors
26. Ann's (Kensington Lighting Co.)
27. Antiquarius
28. Apter-Fredericks
29. Artemis Decorative Arts
30. Baumkotter Gallery
31. Bonhams Knightsbridge
32. Joanna Booth
33. Butchoff
34. Michael German Antiques
35. Guinevere Antiques
36. Adrian Harrington Rare Books
37. Michael Hughes Antiques
38. Anthony James & Son Ltd
39. The Lacquer Chest
40. London Antiques Gallery
41. S. Marchant & Son
42. Millner Manolatos
43. Pruskin Gallery
44. Puritan Values
45. Rafferty & Walwyn
46. Paul Reeves
47. Reindeer Antiques
48. Brian Rolleston Antiques
49. Patrick Sandberg Antiques
50. Stockspring Antiques
51. Through the Looking Glass
52. Neal Wibroe & Natasha MacIlwaine
53. Jack Casimir
54. Caelt Gallery
55. Hirst Antiques
56. Jones Antique Lighting
57. Lacy Gallery
58. Portobello Market
59. Tribal Gathering London
60. Sean Arnold Sporting Antiques
61. David Black Carpets
62. Craven Gallery
63. Claire Guest Ltd
64. The Mark Gallery
65. The Clock Clinic Ltd
66. Hanshan Tang Books
67. AZ Persian Carpet Gallery
68. N. Courlander Ltd.
69. Gregory and Co. Jewellers
70. Horton
71. W & A Houben
72. Edwardian Fireplace Co
73. Just a Second
74. Lloyds International Auction Galleries
75. Thornhill Galleries
76. Cobb Antiques
77. Merton Abbey Mills Market
78. W.F. Turk

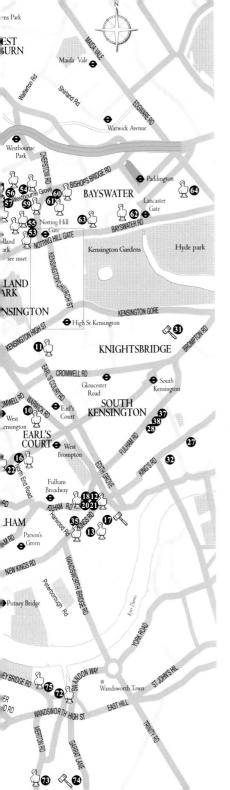

West London

West and north of the River Thames are some smart suburbs, and also many of the best-quality antique shops in London. There are several worthy shops in and around Knightsbridge, and a great many on the New King's Road, on towards Fulham. The Fulham Road and, to the north, Kensington Church Street, are especially rich in antique offerings. West along Kensington High Street is Olympia, its Exhibition Centre an important destination for antique shows. Further north lies Notting Hill Gate, home to the world-famous Portobello Road antique market. Beyond is charming Chiswick and, further south, prosperous Barnes.

Barnes

This verdant and spacious suburb is situated south-west of London's centre, yet it is well served by bus and rail transport: it is a good prospect for the antique shopper. Basically two adjoining postal districts – SW13 (Mortlake) and SW14 (East Sheen) – this area is prosperous and much favoured by actors and TV personalities. It sits in a great loop of the River Thames, west of Hammersmith, and is blessed with wide, green spaces. There is a good selection of antique shops here, especially along White Hart Lane.

Christine Bridge

78 Castelnau, SW13　*　020 8255 0172　*　www.antiqueglass.co.uk　*　Tube: Hammersmith; Bus: 33, 72, 209, 283　*　By appointment 'at any time'

Antique shop: glassware, ceramics, bronzes, needlework

A mixture of styles, unusual objects and decorative items is sold at this intriguing shop. Christine Bridge loves glass, and she has plenty of 18th- and 19th-century examples on show, some of high quality, often engraved and coloured. Ceramics, smaller decorative items, bronzes and needlework are also sold. The shop offers various services, from glass polishing to de-clouding. Valuation and shipping services are offered as well.

Mary Cooke

121 Mortlake High Street (at the Old Power Station), SW14　*　020 8876 5777　*　e-mail: silver@marycooke.co.uk　*　Mainline rail: Mortlake; Bus: 419, 485, 209　*　By appointment only

Specialist antique shop: assorted silver pieces

This is a specialist place for the silver enthusiast, for the only articles here are crafted of that beautiful metal, and in a variety of forms. There is a good deal to see here, from spoons to large vases, coming from most periods and several countries. Valuation and restoration services.

The Dining Room Shop

62-64 White Hart Lane, SW13 * **020 8878 1020** *
www.thediningroomshop.co.uk * **Tube: Hammersmith; Bus:
209** * **Mon–Sat 10:00–17:30; Sun by appointment**

Large shop: dining-room furniture and furnishings from the 18th century

A large and well laid-out place with lots of material and furniture allied to the art
of dining. There are sets of country and more formal furnishings from the 18th century onwards. A host of dining-related items is also for sale, from glassware to china,
cutlery to pottery, and antique lace to damask table linens. Some small decorative
items, too. Valuations, restorations, and an interior decorating service are on offer.

Tables with intricate inlays can be found at The Dining Room Shop.

Chiswick

This leafy settlement lies just beyond Hammersmith, and has a charming and quiet Thames frontage. Walk along the waterside path from Hammersmith Bridge for a scenic route. Chiswick has a business centre, but is most notable for its handsome Thames-side streets; many of the Edwardian and Victorian houses here are lived in by professionals with families, who favour the area for its green spaces. Chiswick House, built in 1729, is an example of a Palladian-style country palace: beautiful, elegant and spare, with a walled park.

Chiswick Fireplace Co.

68 Southfield Road, W4 * 020 8995 4011 * www.thechiswickfireplace.co.uk * Tube: Turnham Green; Bus: E3 * Mon–Sat 09:30 – 17:00

Showroom: Victorian and Edwardian fireplaces

For those who have acquired one of London's many 19th-century houses, this is an ideal place to find a fireplace. This sizeable showroom offers a range of authentic Victorian and Edwardian, mostly cast-iron fireplaces. The surrounds are of tile, wood and stone, sometimes framed in more cast iron. The grander examples have marble and limestone frames. Installation and restoration services provided.

David Edmonds

1-4 Prince of Wales Terrace, W4 * 020 8742 1920 * e-mail: dareindia@aol.com * Tube: Turnham Green; Bus: 27, 190, 267 * Mon–Sat 10:00 – 17:00, Sun by appointment

Large showrooms: antiques and architectural items from India and the sub-continent

A rare and very special shop, as all its stock is from India and the sub-continent. It's a big place, and the space is needed, because although there are some small antiques and architectural items, many are large. Pieces are made from traditional materials – wood, clay, stone – and prices vary. Restoration and valuation services.

Marshall Phillips

38-40 Chiswick Lane, W4 * 020 8742 8089 *
www.marshallphillips.com * Tube: Turnham Green;
Bus: 237, 261, 391 * Mon–Fri 9:30–17:00, Sat 9:30–16:00

Antique shop: French antique furniture and furnishings, garden furniture and statuary

The speciality here is French antique furniture, chandeliers, wall lights and lanterns, as well as objects in bronze and porcelain. Garden furniture and statuary is a special interest, with a wide range of items and prices. Special services include oil and water gilding, casting and patination. Valuations and restoration services offered.

The Old Cinema, Antiques Department Store

16 Chiswick High Road, W4 * 020 8995 4166 *
www.theoldcinema.co.uk * Tube: Turnham Green; Buses H91,
27, 237, 267 * Mon–Sat 10:00–18:00, Sun 12:00–17:00

Antique department store: garden sculpture, architectural items, furniture

Yes indeed, of the many uses London's 'between the wars' film palaces have been put to, this is indeed unusual – a department store of antiquities. The stock here is wide-ranging, with an accent on the period spanning the 17th to the mid-20th centuries. There are garden sculptures, architectural items and varied decorations, but also plenty of furniture. Delivery and restoration services.

Oriental Furniture and Arts

24 Devonshire Road, W4 * 020 8987 8571 * Tube: Turnham
Green; Bus: 27, 190, 267 * Mon–Sat 10:00–17:00

Antique shop: a wide-ranging stock of Oriental antiques

A considerable and wide-ranging stock of Oriental antiques from several centuries is sold here. Chinese furniture of the 18th century is emphasized, but modern pieces are sold too, along with ancient pottery and tomb figures. A fascinating shop.

Strand Antiques

46 Devonshire Road, W4 * **020 8994 1912** * **Tube: Turnham Green; Bus: 27, 190, 267** * **Tues–Sat 10:30–17:30**

Antique shop: furniture, lighting, glassware, ceramics

You are stepping into a French world here, with its pleasing air of a 'brocante'. There are quite a few English antiques, too, however, from furniture to lighting. Other areas of interest here include glass, ceramics, jewellery, silver, prints and books. There is also a range of old garden items, as well as antique textiles and kitchenware.

Services

The London Antique Restoration Services Ltd
4 Wilson Walk, Prebend Gardens, W4 * **020 8846 9709** *
Tube: Turnham Green; Bus: 27, 190 * **Mon–Fri 09:00–17:00**

Work carried out includes re-upholstery, furniture repair, lighting design and restoration of a range of chandeliers, lanterns, table lamps, wall lights and sconces. Mirror and picture-frame restoration is undertaken as well.

While you're in the area... CHISWICK HOUSE

Burlington Lane, W4 * **020 8995 0508** * **www.english-heritage.org.uk** * **Tube: Turnham Green; Bus: 190, E3** * **Open April–Sept 10:00–18:00, Sat 10:00–14:00; October 10:00–17:00; Nov–Mar pre-booked tours and hospitality only** * **Admission fee**

Built in the 18th century in 17th-century Italianate style by the Earl of Burlington, this structure is arguably one of the most glorious examples of the architecture of the time. Lord Burlington was an early visitor on a Grand Tour to Italy, and was influenced by the elegant designs of the famed architect and artist, Andrea Palladio, who had built many villas in the area around the northern town of Vicenza. Don't miss the Blue Velvet Room, with its gilded decorations and intricate ceiling panels.

Earl's Court

With good local shopping and some handsome streets and garden squares, this is mainly a residential area – and yet there are many small hotels here. Defined by the always busy Earl's Court Road, this is a part of London long used to taking in new arrivals. For some time the area was popular with Australians; now there are many Eastern Europeans living within its confines. At one time it was a good spot for antiques shops, but alas, now there are few.

Beaver Coin Room

Beaver Hotel, 57 Philbeach Gardens, SW5 * 020 7373 4555 * e-mail: hotelbeaver@hotmail.com * Tube: Earls Court, West Kensington; Bus: 74, 328, C1 * By appointment only

Coin shop: European coinage, some dating to the 10th century; commemorative medallions

This small coin shop is unusual in that, unlike so many that really only have relatively recent examples, the stock here includes coins dating back to the 10th century. The focus is on European coinage. Commemorative medallions are also interesting, with examples from the 15th century to the 20th. This business has been established for over 35 years, and there is always someone to give helpful advice when needed, and valuations as well.

Orsini Period Clothing

76 Earls Court Road, W8 * 020 7937 2903 * e-mail: info@vintageclothing-london.co.uk * Tube: Earls Court; Bus: 74, 328, C1 * Mon–Sat 12:00 – 18:00

Clothing shop: glamorous vintage clothing

This is a well-established company specializing in 'glamorous Hollywood-style' clothing, including evening gowns, dresses, corsets, fur jackets and beaded dresses from the 1920s to the 1960s. Owner Constantino di Trocchio travels all over the country sourcing these amazing costumes and accessories.

Fulham and World's End

Fulham is extensive, residential and very smart, encompassing both Chelsea and South Kensington. The road at its Knightsbridge beginning heads towards the western section of Fulham. The area is renowned for its long main artery, the Fulham Road, which runs between Chelsea and South Kensington, paralleling an area called World's End, home to a large number of fashion outlets, art galleries and antique shops, some of very good quality. Then comes Fulham itself, a one-time London village. Also here are the Lillie and North End roads, two crowded thoroughfares that bisect each other just beyond the Earl's Court's exhibition halls, with all sorts of local shops in a run-down but very friendly quarter.

The Amphora

340 Fulham Road, SW10 * 020 737 4808 * Tube: Fulham Broadway; Bus: 14, 414, 424 * Mon–Sat 09:30 – 17:00

Corner shop: Vases, urns, decorated pots, garden ornaments

A single-storey corner shop with faded boards announcing its name, this shop is distinctly tatty, but interesting – it is literally stuffed with all sorts of vases, urns and decorated pots in a variety of colours and materials, as well as natural terracotta. Also on sale are sculptures and garden ornaments.

Birdie Fortescue

Cooper House, Unit GJ, 2 Michael Road, SW6 * 01206 337 557 * www.birdiefortescue.com * Tube: Fulham Broadway; Bus: 11, 211 * By appointment only

Antique shop: Art Déco vases, silver, pottery items, furniture, accessories

A fine and wide-ranging collection of antiquities, yet most notable for its superior Art Déco vases, silver and pottery items; furniture, including some unusual mirrors; decorative accessories and other 1920s and 1930s objets d'art. For serious collectors of this fashionable era, it's worth checking the website for current acquisitions.

Decorative Antiques

284 Lillie Road SW6 * **020 7610 2694** * **Tube: Baron's Court; Fulham Broadway; Bus: 74, 190, 430** * **Mon–Sat 10:30–17:30**

Antique shop: French country furniture and accessories of the 18th century

A handsome shop with an unusual stock: French country furniture and accessories of the 18th century. This newly fashionable, often charmingly simple style is quite hard to find in fine examples – in aristocratic France, life swung around Versailles, and it was a disgrace to be banished to the country, and thus a deadly life away from court. Hence, there are not too many good examples of this aesthetic, making a visit here doubly interesting. Valuations and restorations.

Fulham Cross Antiques

318-320 Munster Road, SW6 * **020 7610 3644** * **Tube: Barons Court; Bus: 424** * **Mon–Sat 10:00–17:30**

Antique shop: furniture specialist with 18th- and 19th-century English and European examples

An antique furniture specialist, with good 18th- and 19th-century examples from England and Europe on display. Additional interest is expressed in gilded furniture and mirrors, as well as some lacquered and painted pieces: such delicate period items, usually French or Italian, are rare. Restoration work is also carried out.

The Furniture Shop

248 North End Road, SW6 * **020 7381 9399** * **Tube: West Brompton; Bus: 28, 391** * **Wed–Sat 10:30–18:00, Tues 14:30–18:00,**

Household shop: furniture, pottery, rugs, bric-à-brac

Literally stuffed with items, these three high-ceilinged spaces stand side by side under a block of flats. There's a huge range of stuff here, a lot of it household furniture and oddities, from pottery seven dwarves to old trunks. Some of the stuff for sale here is indeed junk, however, you are encouraged to poke around by the affable woman in charge. Some worthwhile articles can be found, including French chairs, Edwardian tables, rugs and tapestries. Restoration workshop.

155

Lots Road Auctions

71-73 Lots Road, SW10 * **020 7376 6800** * **www.lotsroad.com**
* **e-mail: info@lotsroad.com** * **Tube: Fulham Broadway; Bus:
11** * **Contemporary and Traditional Furnishings Auction held
every Sun at 13:00; Antique Furniture, Pictures, Carpets and
Works of Art Auction held every Sun at 16:00; Open for
viewing Thursday 10:00—19:00, Friday 09:00—14:00, Saturday
10:00—16:00, and Sunday 10:00—13:00.**

Auction house: antiques and memorabilia

Ride down the King's Road to its junction beyond World's End and you will come
to Lots Road, just off to the left. Halfway down on the right of this main street leading to Chelsea Harbour is an auction house in a modern building. Regular auctions
of antiques and interesting memorabilia are listed on notices in its windows, and
some items are on show for upcoming themed sales. Call to obtain information, or
request to be placed on their mailing list.

Lucy Johnson

10 Billing Place SW10 * **020 7352 0114** *
www.lucy-johnson.com * **Tube: Fulham Broadway;
Bus: 14, 414, 424** * **By appointment only**

Antique shop: Tudor and early 17th-century pieces, hangings, tapestries

It's unusual to find such a place anywhere, specializing as it does in such fine early
English furniture, plus small articles in metal and local wood such as oak and walnut of similar provenance. Much of it must already be in museums. This fascinating,
atmospheric shop, with its well-placed items, shows a range of Tudor and early 17th-
century tables, storage chests, dressers, chairs, stools and other rare pieces, alongside
hangings and tapestries. Candlestands and decorative items from plaques to wall
sconces are also sold. Online gallery.

Bidding can become intense at Lots Road Auctions, one of London's valued smaller auction houses.

Numbers 275, 291 & 313 Antiques

275, 291 and 313 Lillie Road, SW6 * 020 7386 7382, 020 7381 5009, and 020 7610 2380 * **Tube: Barons Court, Fulham Broadway; Bus: 74, 190, 430** * **All open Mon–Fri 10:00–17:30**

*A **cluster of antique shops**: 17th- to 19th-century English and European antiquities; statuary; paintings*

These three elegant shops sit very close together, strung along Lillie Road (at the Fulham end), and making a smart enclave in an otherwise dull and ordinary thoroughfare. The stock here varies from 17th- to 19th-century English and European antiquities to 19th-century Gothic-style pieces. Also on show are garden statuary, oil and watercolour paintings, carpets and various decorative items, and even 1960s Lucite pieces and lamps. A nice variety of styles and eras, as well as various services in these attractive premises.

The Parson's Table

362 Fulham Road, SW10 * 020 7352 7444 * **e-mail: parsonstable@btopenworld.com** * **Tube: Fulham Broadway; Bus: 14, 414, 424** * **Mon–Fri 10:00–17:30, but call first**

Large shop/workroom: 19th-century furnishings

The green-framed window of this dusty establishment looks out onto a curve of the street. A large workroom lies beyond the street window, with a variety of pieces crammed together. Lots of 19th-century furnishings here, both large and small, and also dining and side chairs, both in pairs and in sets. There are also various tables and big gilt mirrors.

Stephen Long Antiquarian & Secondhand Bookseller

348 Fulham Road, SW10 * 020 7352 8810 * **Tube: Fulham Broadway; Bus: 14, 414, 424** * **Mon–Sat 10:00–17:30**

Bookshop: Roman Catholic theology

This is a light and airy shop, with a big window at the back opening to a formal town garden; it has been run for 13 years by a friendly couple. The speciality of his shop, explains Mr Long, is unusual – Roman Catholic theology. There are many other antiquarian books, however, packed on shelves and even piled on the floor.

Treasure Island

**127 Lillie Road, SW6
✲ 020 7385 1913 ✲
Tube: Barons Court,
Fulham Broadway;
Bus: 28, 391 ✲
Mon–Sat 11:00 – 18:00**

*Junk shop: unusual
bric-à-brac, from modern to
more dated*

The shelves at Stephen Long are laden with antiquarian books on a variety of subjects.

Near North End Road, this is a small junk shop jammed with stuff. The affable American owner is a transplant from New York State, and happily discusses his bizarre range of stock. Items are dominated by modern stuff at the door, such as electric kettles and record players, though there can be more unusual things, too. Penetrate into the interior, however, and search for treasures: paintings, brass fittings and lamps, tapestries, old bottles, vases – there's a motley lot here.

Hammersmith

Hammersmith has many hidden attributes, so don't be put off by the frantic traffic circle. There is a lively High Street and a wonderful fruit and vegetable street market nearby on North End Road (Mon–Sat from 09:00). A short distance away is the River Thames, crossed by a Victorian bridge, with old, stately houses lining its banks.

Architectural Antiques

351 & 324 King Street, W6 * 020 8741 7883 * www.aa-fireplaces.co.uk * Tube: Hammersmith; Bus: 27, 190, 267, 391 * Mon–Fri 08:30 – 16:30

Multiple showrooms: marble and other stone fireplaces and surrounds

The stock here is mostly marble and stone fireplaces and surrounds, including English and European chimneypieces and a selection of architectural and decorative artefacts.

Paravent

Flat 10, Ranelagh Gardens, Stamford Brook Avenue, W6 * 020 8748 6323 * www.paravent.co.uk * Tube: Stamford Brook; Bus: 11, 237 * By appointment only

Showroom: antique screens

A source for magnificent 17th- to 20th-century screens from all over the world. They will also source particular screens for customers. Restorations are done here as well.

Rochtel Interiors

72 Fulham Palace Road, W6 * 020 8741 5626 * Tube: Hammersmith; Bus: 74, 220, 430 * Mon–Fri 10:00 – 18:00, Sat 10:00 – 13:30

Shop: soft furnishings

This shop specializes in modern soft furnishings such as curtains, cushion covers, throws, pelmets and tie-backs, with some antiques for sale as well.

Kensington

One of the smartest of London's neighbourhoods, this is a place where the wealthy and famous live. Its leafy purlieus extend from Hyde Park westwards, and its edge is marked by Kensington Palace. The main artery and central Tube station is Kensington High Street. The primary concentration of shops here are thickly clustered all the way up Kensington Church Street, right up to Notting Hill Gate. Towards the river, the area becomes South Kensington, and here, along the King's and Fulham roads, as they run parallel, a selection of high-quality antique shops are lined up, shoulder to shoulder.

Ann's (Kensington Lighting Company)

Two locations: 34a and 34b, and 59 Kensington Church Street, W8 * 020 7937 5915 * e-mail: kensingtonlight@btconnect.com * Tube: Kensington High Street, Notting Hill Gate; Bus: 27, 28, 52, 70, 328 * Mon–Sat 09:00 – 17:30

Showrooms: reproduction lamps, lights, chandeliers, shades

A glittering Aladdin's cave of lighting, but despite appearances and the many and various styles here, all these examples are skillful, well finished reproductions. Nevertheless, they would complement antique furnishings well. Many kinds and styles of lighting are sold in both locations: reading and standing lamps, table lamps, wall lights and brackets. Chandeliers can also be found amidst the forest of lights hanging from the ceiling. A range of handmade shades is for sale as well. Cheerful help.

Antiquarius

131–141 King's Road, SW3 * 020 7351 5353 * Tube: Sloane Square; Bus: 11, 19, 22, 211, 319 * Mon–Sat 10:00 – 18:00

Antique centre: vintage clothing, furniture, books, glassware, jewellery, porcelain, textiles, timepieces

A mammoth antique centre offering dozens of specialist dealers in an ideal location at King's Road and Flood Street. Items for sale include vintage clothing, antique furniture, lighting, books, glassware, jewellery, porcelain, textiles and timepieces.

Apter-Fredericks

265–267 Fulham Road, SW3 * **020 7352 2188** *
www.apter-fredericks.com * **Tube: South Kensington; Bus: 14, 211, 414** * **Mon–Fri 9:30 – 17:30, other times by appointment**

Antique shop: English 18th- and 19th-century furniture and accessories

This is a spectacular shop, its gold and white theatrically framed street windows making it look like a stage, revealing in their glow a cave of extravagant and expensive delights for those who appreciate the very best English antique furniture. A stunningly beautiful shop inside, too. Sold here are mostly 18th- and 19th-century pieces, plus accessories of the first quality, with period bibelots impeccably arranged.

Artemis Decorative Arts

36 Kensington Church Street, W8 * **020 7376 0377** *
www.artemisdecorativearts.com * **Tube: Kensington High Street, Notting Hill Gate; Bus: 27, 28, 52, 70, 328** * **Mon–Fri 10:00 – 17:30, Sat 11:00 – 17:00**

Antique shop: glassware, porcelain, decorative arts

There is a considerable array of well chosen and elegant articles in this pale, airy shop. On show is some splendid glass (including some fine decanters) and porcelain, with big names such as Lalique and Gallé represented. 'Our range of the decorative arts continues into Art Déco and right up to the 1940s', informs the owner. The range includes lamps, pottery, vases, and there's a defined accent on the 1930s, with objects ranging from ivory to bakelite. A few prints dot the otherwise bare walls.

Baumkotter Gallery

63a Kensington Church Street * **020 7937 5171** *
www.baumkottergallery.com * **Tube: Kensington High Street, Notting Hill Gate; Bus: 27, 28, 52, 70, 328** *
Mon–Fri 10:30 – 6:30; Sat & Sun by appointment

Apter Fredericks is renowned for the great beauty and excellent quality of its carefully chosen selection of 18th-century English furniture.

Gallery: 17th- to 21st-century oil paintings

An arts firm for over 40 years, with the mother of present owner Nicholas Baumkotter before him, plus a 20 years' residence on the Kensington Church Street front, this gallery has plans to move to Cheam, in Surrey. (The owners may be contacted for current stock, and many items are pictured on the website.) The gallery deals in 'fine 17th- to 21st-century oil paintings', and it offers a wide-ranging collection of mostly classical oils, the pictures representing a large variety of styles and schools. It also has some handsome frames, mostly modern and a few antique ones, too.

Bonhams, Knightsbridge

13 Montpelier Street, SW7 * 020 7393 3900 * www.bonhams.com * Tube: Knightsbridge; Bus: C1, 14, 74, 414 * Open Sat & Sun for viewing only; see website for auction dates and viewing times * Other location: 101 New Bond Street, W1S * 020 7629 6602

Auction rooms: various items for sale

This is the second branch of Bonhams in London (the other is in Mayfair), and here you'll find auctions of all kinds. From vintage cars and automobilia to Old Masters paintings, along with portrait miniatures, prints, furniture, clocks, watches, objets d'art, tribal art, musical instruments, guns and antiquities. A general valuation service is also provided.

Joanna Booth

247 King's Road, SW3 * 020 7352 8998 * www.joannabooth.co.uk * Tube: South Kensington; Bus: 14, 211, 414 * Mon–Fri: 10:00–18:00, or by appointment Sat and evenings

Antique shop: Gothic sculpture, carvings, Old Masters' works, needlework

Established over 40 years ago, this fascinating shop has some splendidly impressive articles, including Gothic sculpture, and other carved pieces up to the 17th century. The works of art for sale include drawings by various Old Masters. The furniture is mostly of early provenance, and there is a tapestry, needlework and fabric section, with fine specimens dating mostly from the 16th and 18th centuries.

Sumptuous tassles, textiles and tapestries from the 18th and 16th centuries adorn the crowded walls at Joanna Booth.

Butchoff

154 Kensington Church Street, W8 * 020 7221 8174 *
www.butchoff.com * **Tube: Kensington High Street, Notting
Hill Gate; Bus: 27, 28, 52, 70, 328** * **Mon–Fri 09:30 – 18:00,
Sat 9:30 – 16:00**

Antique shop: 18th- and 19th-century furniture

These remarkable and elegant premises show splendid examples of 18th- and 19th-
century furniture. There are lots of superb Georgian items, yet the Regency style is
the one much preferred by the owners, who proudly proclaim that the business is 'a
family affair'. From armchairs to clocks, tables to desks, there are also 'after the
Regency' pieces: some florid and some from famous makers, often in styles borrowed
from the previous century. Also stocked are French, Italian and Colonial pieces. A
well-researched catalogue of current examples is regularly issued.

Michael German Antiques

38b Kensington Church Street, W8 * 020 7937 2771 *
www.antiquecanes.com * **Tube: Kensington High Street,
Notting Hill Gate; Bus: 27, 28, 52, 70, 328** *
Mon–Sat 10:00 – 18:00

Antique shop: miniature war armament, walking sticks

A rare and fascinating special interest here in this tiny shop – miniature cannons,
swords and plated samples, even suits of old European and Oriental armour are
paired with an oddity: the elegant old walking sticks, or canes, that were once used
for town and country promenading and walking, reaching a peak in the 19th
century, when country-house racks must have jostled with them. Many have silver or
brass fittings, as well as exotically sculpted handles of ivory or bone, and look very
elegant displayed in this shop against plum red walls in racks and rows.

Guinevere Antiques

574-580 Kings Road, SW6 * 020 7736 2917 *
www.guinevere.co.uk * **Tube: Fulham Broadway; Bus: 11, 19,
22, 211, 319** * **Mon–Fri 09:30 – 18:00, Sat 10:00 – 17:30**

Showrooms: a vast selection of items, specializing in the rare and unique

146

This vast shop, with its multiple showrooms, is something to see. The furniture and decorative objects within its many rooms are arranged as mis-en-scenes, enabling visitors to envision how the wares might look in their homes. The owners take pride in their unusual, high-quality stock, offering, among other items, goods made from materials that are luxurious but scarce, such as ebony, tortoiseshell, shagreen, ivory and horn. Other items are characterized by clean lines and a strong decorative presence.

Adrian Harrington Rare Books

64a Kensington Church Street, W8 * 020 7937 1465 * e-mail: rare@harringtonbooks.co.uk * Tube: Kensington High Street, Notting Hill Gate; Bus: 27, 28, 52, 70, 328 * Mon–Sat 11:00 – 18:00

Bookshop: sets, first editions, children's, travel, Winston Churchill biographies

This shop has the air of a library, and indeed, fine and rare books are stocked here. The comfortable, warm rooms are lined with them; some even spill in piles on to the parquetry floors. The floor-to-ceiling shelves are loaded with handsomely bound volumes. Sets of books, old and modern, 20th and 21st century, first editions, literature, children's books, voyages and travel are all a speciality, as are books on Winston Churchill. They buy and sell entire libraries, too. Very able assistance from manager Pierre Lombardini.

Michael Hughes Antiques

88 Fulham Road, SW3 * 020 7589 0660 * www.michaelhughesantiques.co.uk * Tube: South Kensington; Bus: 14, 211, 414 * Mon–Fri 09:30 – 17:30, Sat by appointment

Gallery: English furniture of the 18th and 19th centuries

Some spectacular pieces of furniture can be viewed here, notably massive Regency pieces (early 19th century) of fine workmanship in rare woods, often highly decorated and gilded. This era under the Prince Regent's indulgent rule was truly luxurious, and has never gone out of fashion in the UK. The speciality areas in this handsome gallery are 18th- and 19th- century English pieces of particularly fine quality, some French-influenced by known masters. Also sold are works of art and bibelots.

Anthony James & Son Ltd

88 Fulham Road, SW3 * **020 7584 1120** *
www.anthony-james.com * **Tube: South Kensington; Bus: 14,
345, 414** * **Mon–Fri 09:30—17:30, also by appointment**

Antique shop: furniture, bibelots and accessories from various periods

An unusual shop with no particular theme, yet with some memorable fine objects.
Here's the reason: 'We like to sell the things that we enjoy ourselves', says the welcoming Mr James. Hence this tends to be a collection of very personal choices in
furniture, bibelots and accessories. There are indeed, to quote from their card, some
most 'elegant period pieces and decorative objects' here, a selection from quite a
wide-ranging cross-section of dates and times.

The Lacquer Chest

75 Kensington Church Street, W8 * **020 7937 1306** * **Tube:
Kensington High Street, Notting Hill Gate; Bus: 27, 28, 52, 70,
328** * **Mon–Fri 09:30—5:30, Sat 11:00—6:00**

*Old-style shop: 19th- and 20th-century material: chairs, chests, clocks,
bibelots*

This is actually one of two shops: the other near-neighbour is at No 71, called
Lacquer Chest Too, with similar wares behind its big square bay window. You can
wander from one shop to the other: both are indicated with gilded street signs.
Comfortably old-style and atmospheric, both shops offer a collection of considerable variety, and not a few oddities. Mostly 19th- and 20th-century material here,
from chairs and chests to clocks and bibelots. Friendly and helpful assistance. Items
can be hired out.

London Antiques Gallery

6e Kensington Church Street, W8 * **020 7229 2934** * **Tube:
Kensington High Street, Notting Hill Gate; Bus: 27, 28, 52, 70,
328** * **Mon–Sat 10:00—18:00**

Gallery: 18th- and 19th-century pottery and porcelains, glassware

A small, elegant corner gallery, this lively clutter of a place really welcomes you in. Here you will find a lot of 18th- and 19th-century pottery and porcelains, both from England and other European origins, and the range goes from Staffordshire figures and 1930s figurines to French and English bisque dolls, 19th-century glasses and fine decanters.

S. Marchant & Son

120 Kensington Church Street, W8 * **020 7229 5319** * www.marchantasianart.com * **Tube: Kensington High Street, Notting Hill Gate; Bus: 27, 28, 52, 70, 328** * **Mon–Fri 09:30 – 18:00**

Antique shop: Oriental art, porcelains, furnishings

This family firm has been in this location since the 1950s. Inside, the well ordered room has a flight of steps at the rear which takes you to a higher level: you look past polished mahogany window frames into a cream-carpeted interior flanked with sprays of orchids. The fine Oriental pieces stand out well in their frames against a plummy maroon background. Japanese and Chinese porcelains are placed on side tables (these and accompanying furnishings are also for sale).

Millner Manolatos

2 Campden Street, W8 * **020 7229 3268** * www.millnermanolatos.com * **Tube: Kensington High Street, Notting Hill Gate; Bus: 27, 28, 52, 70, 328** * **Tues–Fri 12:00 – 18:00, Sat 12:00 – 16:30, other times by appointment**

Gallery: Asian and Indian stone statues, friezes, cabinetwork, textiles

This is a gallery of unique treasures for anyone with an interest in Asian antiques. Exceptionally unusual Indian pieces here, from stone statues of gods to wooden sculptures, white marble pillar capitals and carved friezes. Many Northern Indian exotic examples include birds as part of oil lamps and extraordinary cabinets and chests in ornate gold designs. Ottoman tiles and inscribed Egyptian panels are also sold, as are pieces from Syria, Mesopotamia, Thailand and Java. There are Greek textiles and 19th-century pictures, too, as well as drawings. Regular illustrated catalogues are issued.

Pruskin Gallery

73 Kensington Church Street, W8 * 020 7937 1994 * e-mail: pruskin@pruskingallery.com * Tube: Kensington High Street, Notting Hill Gate; Bus: 27, 28, 52, 70, 328 * Mon–Fri 10:00–18:00, Sat 11:00–17:00

Gallery: late 19th-, early to mid 20th-century decorative art, including pottery, clocks, jewellery, lamps

The show window is laid out with unusual objects carefully spaced on its marble floor. The shop itself is light and white, a foil to the shining Art Déco colours. Although the claim is 'Decorative Art 1880 – 1960', the major accent is on the 1920s and 1930s pieces here, and the owner has gathered together a range of examples, from gleaming pottery to taut little statuettes neatly displayed in this pleasingly chaste shop. Arranged on tables and shelves is a number of odd, mostly 19th-century clocks, jewellery, lamps and bibelots. An array of arresting things to look at.

Puritan Values

69 Kensington Church Street, W8 * 01502 722 211 * www.puritanvalues.com * Tube: Kensington High Street, Notting Hill Gate; Bus: 27, 28, 52, 70 * Mon–Sat 10:00–17:00

Antique shop: rugs, 19th-century arts, naïf-painted and country furniture

This crowded shop has a real 19th-century air to it. It specializes in 19th-century arts from the Arts and Crafts, Egyptian and Gothic Revivals, Anglo-Japanese and Aesthetics movements. There are rugs, 19th-century paintings and prints, naïf-painted furniture, country-style chairs and American clocks, as well as porcelains, dolls' houses and mirrors.

Rafferty & Walwyn

79 Kensington Church Street, W8 * 020 7938 1100 * www.raffertyantiqueclocks.com * Tube: Kensington High Street, Notting Hill Gate; Bus: 27, 28, 52, 70, 328 * Mon–Fri 10:00–18:00

Antique shop: a range of antique timepieces

A fine array of antique timepieces is for sale at Rafferty & Walwyn.

Based here since 1979, this is a specialist shop selling old timepieces. You peer through a black and gold window frame to a dramatically lit interior backed with apricot wallpaper. There is indeed a galaxy of extraordinary old clocks here, from elegant inlaid William and Mary longcase beauties to Regency wall-mounted ones. The range is mostly English, from the 17th up to the early 19th century, and there are quite a few small bracket examples, and metal lantern ones as well. Buyers in the UK get free delivery and installation; door-to-door packing and insured shipping service is offered for customers abroad.

Paul Reeves

32b Kensington Church Street, W8 * 020 7937 1594 * www.paulreeveslondon.com * Tube: Kensington High Street, Notting Hill Gate; Bus: 27, 28, 52, 70, 328 * Mon–Fri 10:00– 17:30

Antique shop: mid- to late 19th-century furniture from the Arts and Crafts movement

'Furniture and artefacts 1860–1960' says the card, and further exploration in this shop, thick with Victorian atmosphere, reveals a special interest not only in general British furnishings, including some rather bizarre Gothic pieces, but very specifically the Arts and Crafts movement of the mid to late 19th century. The owner is always changing his stock. Famous artist- and architect-designed pieces represented here include examples by Voysey, Curtiss and William Burgess.

Reindeer Antiques Ltd

81 Kensington Church Street, W8 * 020 7937 3754 * www.reindeerantiques.co.uk * Tube: Kensington High Street, Notting Hill Gate; Bus: 27, 28, 52, 70, 328 * Mon–Fri 09:30– 18:00, Sat 11:00–17:00

Antique shop: Georgian clocks and furnishings

This handsome, wide-windowed and high-ceilinged corner shop is full of light, showing up well a mixed stock of mostly Georgian clocks, mirrors, dining and side tables, sets of chairs, boxes, candlesticks, chandeliers and lamps, and fire irons, all well spaced and set against a light cream background. The owner, Peter Alexander, also goes for unusual pieces, such as small Canterburys. The principal pieces here are placed on two levels, and are elegant and in good order. Pleasant, helpful service.

Brian Rolleston Antiques Ltd

104a Kensington Church Street, W8 * 020 7229 5892 * Tube: Kensington High Street, Notting Hill Gate; Bus: 27, 28, 52, 70, 328 * Mon–Fri 10:00 – 17:00, Sat by appointment

Antiques shop: 17th- and 18th-century English furniture and furnishings

Beyond a white-framed window, the grey-green carpet in this shop acts as a good foil to the all-English 17th- and 18th-century furniture for sale here, all well displayed. On two levels a range of chests, chairs, tables, brass chandeliers, mirrors and clocks is displayed. The William and Mary examples, often walnut, are of high quality, with the fine marquetry and ornate inlays of the late 17th century on classic bun feet. Sometimes Regency articles such as brass-inlaid dining tables are stocked too, along with period pictures and models of Chinese pagodas.

range of formidable antique shops line both sides of the busy Kensington Church Street.

A neat display of 18th-century English tea caddies at Patrick Sandberg.

Patrick Sandberg Antiques

150-152 Kensington Church Street, London W8 * 020 7229
0373 * www.antiquefurniture.net * Tube: Kensington High
Street, Notting Hill Gate; Bus: 27, 28, 52, 70, 328 * Mon–Fri
10:00 – 18:00, Sat 10:00 – 16:00

Antique shop: fine English furniture and works of art

You can't miss seeing the front of this pretty shop, which looks exactly as you might
imagine an antique shop dealing in 'Fine English Furniture & Works of Art' (as indicated on the card) should look. The well-placed objects in the multi-paned windows
beside the hanging sign invite a closer inspection before you enter from the small
forecourt. Within are examples of classic, mostly 18th-century pieces, and plenty of
small, mostly contemporary items designed to complement them. Some pictures and
prints, books and bibelots are for sale as well.

Stockspring Antiques

114 Kensington Church Street, London W8 * 020 7727 7995
* www.antique-porcelain.co.uk * Tube: Kensington High
Street, Notting Hill Gate; Bus: 27, 28, 52, 70, 328 * Mon–Fri
10:00 – 17:30, Sat 10:00 – 13:00

*Antique shop: English and Continental porcelain, glassware, figurines;
Delft and Chinese ceramics*

A place for lovers of porcelain of the finest quality and styles, this small-fronted
shop – painted dark green with the name set out on its marquee, above tightly packed
window displays – is a must for collectors. On two plainly decorated floors, in simple, bare glass boxes or on shelves, is an array of articles ranging from dinner and tea
services to candlesticks, pots, platters, bowls, urns and vases. Special areas are 18th-
century English and Continental pieces, but there is also glassware, figurines, and
Delft and Chinese ceramics.

Through the Looking Glass

137 Kensington Church Street, W8 * 020 7221 4026 * Tube:
Kensington High Street, Notting Hill Gate; Bus: 27, 28, 52, 70,
328 * Mon–Fri 10:00 – 17:30

Antique shop: mostly 19th-century mirrors

You can hardly get into this shop for the vast array of gleaming mirrors – it feels a bit like the classic child's story of an umbrella shop so crowded that they flew out of the door when it was opened. This is a straightforward shop selling 19th-century mirrors, with nothing else on the walls or stacked: there's a fantastic collection here, from huge ones with rococo or classical frames, to concave examples (almost all are gilded), and to smaller ornate or plain examples. If you want an antique mirror of whatever size, you can hardly fail to find it here.

Neal Wibroe & Natasha MacIlwaine

77 Kensington Church Street, W8 ＊ 020 7937 2461 ＊ Tube: Kensington High Street, Notting Hill Gate; Bus: 27, 28, 52, 70, 328 ＊ Mon–Fri 10:00–17:30, Sat by appointment

Antique shop: Period furniture and works of art; glassware, lighting fixtures

English desks and cabinets are specialities at Patrick Sandberg's elegant shop.

'Fine period furniture & works of art' states the plain white business card, and that, along with a taste of elegance, is what you get here. On two levels, beside walls hung with prints, is a selection of essentially English 18th-century and fine Regency furniture. There are stylish, gilded and plain-framed mirrors, oak and mahogany desks, corner cupboards and boxes alongside dining and casual chairs of good quality. Smaller items, including glassware and plates, are also sold. Lighting fixtures, sconces and candlesticks are on offer here, too.

Kew

Few antique shops can be found in this leafy area, but Kew has given antique-lovers a gift of a different sort. Here, in 1978, many trees fell during a great storm: inevitably some were rare and very old. In the aftermath of this tragedy, however, there was a bonus: restorers and furniture-makers gained a chance to buy the logs and branches of these old retainers, and thereby came into a new supply of rare veneers from the fallen. The trees thus live on in the restoration of many a wooden antique with these rare, choice woods.

Dinan & Chighine

PO Box 266, TW9 *
020 8948 1939 * by
appointment only

Fairs: 17th- to 19th-century works of art

This dealer is not a shop, but rather, an exhibitor at main fairs, where she shows a large collection of 17th- to 19th-century works of art. If you happen to enjoy the subtle beauties of watercolour art, here you will find some lovely examples of flower paintings, tropical and natural history subjects. Oriental works, classical engravings and hand-coloured prints are for sale, too. Prints can be framed to order.

While you're in the area...
ROYAL BOTANICAL GARDENS

TW9 * 020 8332 5655 * www.rbgkew.org.uk * Tube: Kew Gardens; Bus: 65, 237, 267 * Mon–Fri 09:30 – 17:30, Sat & Sun 09:30 – 19:00 * Admission fee

These extensive gardens always have something to show, whatever the season, their fabled collections of plants and trees, exotic old glass greenhouses and the 18th-century Chinese Pagoda all looking across the River Thames to the regal Syon House.

Notting Hill Gate

The name Notting Hill Gate comes from a toll-gate that stood at Pembridge Road until 1864. Now an expensive, smart area, Notting Hill Gate contains the famous Portobello Road within its borders, which runs from Chepstow Villas to Golborne Road: about a dozen street blocks. Along this road is the Portobello Market, a very important antique destination. Long and curving, the market is lined with small shops and stalls, its untidy length culminating in a fruit and vegetable market. Cutting across Portobello Road is Westbourne Grove, a shopping thoroughfare with a number of good galleries, small antique shops, and markets along and just off it.

Jack Casimir

23 Pembridge Road, W11 * 020 7727 8643 * Tube: Ladbroke Grove or Notting Hill Gate; Bus: 7, 12, 23, 27, 28, 31, 52, 70, 94, 148, 328 * Mon–Sat 10:00—17:30, or by appointment

Antique shop: 17th- and 18th-century copper, brass and pewter

A window on the street glittering with highly polished metal objects set against red walls, this is a specialist shop for those keen on copper, pewter or brass objects of two to three hundred years ago. Jack Casimir specializes in 17th- and 18th-century copper, brass and pewter in a number of uses, from carriage lamps to door plates. There is an array of fireplace articles, grates, scuttles, accessories and equipment, as well as candlesticks, chandeliers and umbrella stands.

Caelt Gallery

182 Westbourne Grove, W11 * 020 7229 9309 * www.caeltgallery.com * Tube: Ladbroke Grove or Notting Hill Gate; Bus: 7, 12, 23, 27, 28, 31, 52, 70, 94, 148, 328 * Mon–Sat 09:30—18:00, Sun 10:30—18:00

Gallery: genuinely eccentric: Soviet works, English portraits and posters

From the two mangy stuffed tigers lounging in the dusty window space to the large

A splendidly dramatic showcase window marks the Jack Casimir shop.

stern pictures of Lenin, you just know this is a genuinely eccentric gallery. Other Russian influences are here too, with examples of Soviet academicians' works beside English country-house portraits, pictures of children, and early 19th-century works and abstracts.

Hirst Antiques

59 Pembridge Road, W11 * **020 7727 9364** * **Tube: Notting Hill Gate; Bus: 31, 328** * **Mon–Sat 11:00 – 18:00**

Antique shop: an eclectic hotchpotch

This shop, standing on a corner, is like a theatre set, with its pair of well-lit windows and two rooms inside as stuffed with glittering items as a magpie's nest. Peer through the doorway and you see chandeliers with crystal drops, draperies over a four-poster bed, embroidered vestments, tapestries, classical busts in marble and metal and showers of jewellery. It's a charming, eclectic hotchpotch. The business is over 40 years old, and is a delightful example of an old-style antiques shop.

Jones Antique Lighting

194 Westbourne Grove, W11 * **020 7229 6866** * **www.jonesantiquelighting.com** * **Tube: Ladbroke Grove or Notting Hill Gate; Bus: 7, 12, 23, 27, 28, 31, 52, 70, 94, 148, 328** * **Mon–Sat 09:30 – 18:00**

Antique shop: lamps and lighting, costume jewellery

An old-fashioned sort of a shop, with its sparkling double-fronted window inviting you into a cavern of colour and light. This is a place to go for all kinds of lamps and lighting, as evidenced by the sconces on the walls and the chandeliers raining down light from the ceiling in a shower of amps. The glass is all old, ranging from 1880, the decade when electric light arrived, to 1940. An additional aspect is a wide range of costume jewellery.

Lacy Gallery

203 Westbourne Grove, W11 * **020 7229 6340** * **Tube: Ladbroke Grove or Notting Hill Gate; Bus: 7, 12, 23, 27, 28, 31, 52, 70, 94, 148, 328** * **Tues–Fri 10:00 – 17:00, Sat 10:00 – 16:00**

Gallery: old pictures up to the mid-20th century

This delightful gallery makes you feel as if you are back in the 19th century. Echoing wooden floors and wide-stepped stairs (there are three floors, the top one lit by a skylight) take you around a host of old pictures, mostly up to the mid-20th century, some 19th and earlier. There is also a good selection of frames, some simple, some ornate, some mirrored, many of them antiquities themselves, along with any number of oddities. They offer a framing service, and the staff is very helpful.

Portobello Market

Portobello Road, W10 & W11 * www.portobelloroad.co.uk * Tube: Ladbroke Grove or Notting Hill Gate; Bus: 7, 12, 23, 27, 28, 31, 52, 70, 94, 148, 328 * Market open Sat 05:30—17:00, many shops are also open Mon–Sat

Market: A winding road of shops and arcades selling all kinds of antiques

Portobello Road provides one of the best-known sites for antique shoppers: the Portobello Market. It started in 1950 at stall 115, and is now a magnet for bargain seekers, with over 1,500 dealers selling virtually every kind of antique and collectable. Saturday is the big market day, while many shops are open six days a week. The trading on Saturdays begins at around 5:30am, when the dealers and serious buyers come out; the crowds come later. Most stall-holders have arrived by 08:00, and trading continues all day. Saturdays at the market are very crowded, while 'other days it can be completely empty', said the owner of one stall. The market winds down to a daily fruit and vegetable local market at the far end. Along its length, local bakers, butchers and small cafés manage to hang out their signs. An information booth is situated at the junction of Portobello Road and Westbourne Grove to direct enquirers to specialist dealers, and for general information. You can ask them for a map listing all of the street's establishments and sidewalk participants. A small selection of shops and stalls is listed below, but it's worth meandering along the road and popping into wherever takes your fancy.

ALICE'S
86 Portobello Road, W11 * 020 7229 8187 * Tues–Fri 09:00—17:00, Sat 07:00—16:00

A treasure trove, this eye-catching red storefront houses a plethora of old and reproduction advertising signs, painted furniture, pond yachts and decorative pieces.

BARHAM ANTIQUES
83 Portobello Road, W11 * 020 7727 3845 * www.barhamantiques.co.uk * Mon–Fri 10:30–17:00, Sat 07:30–17:00

A selection of Victorian and Georgian items, including writing boxes, tea caddies, inkwells and stands, glass épergnes, clocks, paintings, furniture and jewellery boxes.

CENTRAL GALLERY (PORTOBELLO)
125 Portobello Road, W11 * 020 7243 8027 * www.centralgallery.com * Sat 06:00–15:00

A mini-market housing over 25 dealers, there are lots of treasures to be found in this arcade. Stock includes all manner of jewellery from the 18th century to the 1960s, from cameos to coral, and from Art Déco to Victorian silver and gold.

CROWN ARCADE
119 Portobello Road, W11 * 020 7436 9416 * www.portobello-antiques.co.uk * Sat 05:30–15:00

This medium-sized arcade, with its 25 stalls, sits near the corner of Westbourne Grove. For sale here are mostly decorative objects, including glass, bronzes, sculpture, boxes, humidors, decorative prints and decanters.

DAVID'S BOXES
115 Portobello Road, W11 * 020 7243 0464 * e-mail: david@davidsboxes.demon.co.uk * Fri & Sat 12:00–20:00

A great plethora of boxes in a multitude of materials makes up the entire stock here. In this neat showroom are all kinds, from plain to decorative. These 18th- and 19th-century containers were made for many uses. Thus you had caddies for tea (tea used to be locked away in times when it was an expensive commodity), sewing boxes, jewel caskets, writing slopes, and a number of cigar cabinets and humidors. Restoration of old boxes and a leather lining service.

DEMETZY BOOKS
113 Portobello Road, W11 * 01993 702209 * e-mail: demetzybooks@ntlworld.com * Sat 07:30–15:30

A dealer in antiquarian books from the 18th and 19th centuries. The selection is vast, from Dickens first editions to illustrated children's books. Valuations done.

DRUCE ANTIQUES LTD
115 Portobello Road, W11 * 020 7419 5080 * e-mail:
druce_antiques@hotmail.com * Fri–Sat 12:00–20:00

Basically an intriguing place for antique silver and glass – with a special interest in
old napkin rings. A useful shop for those looking for small, unusual gifts. You are
likely to find many unique items here, from coasters to crystal, with some articles in
antique ivory and bone, and metal and wood. Unusually, there is also a range of pairs
of decanters and drinking glasses, both plain and coloured. It's not easy to find a
glass restoration service, but they offer that, too. Very helpful service.

THE HARRIS'S ARCADE
161-163 Portobello Road, W11 * 020 7727 5242 *
www.portobello-antiques.co.uk * Fri & Sat 07:00–15:00

Over 40 dealers are present in this newly renovated arcade space. Here you will find
dealers selling general antiquities, including bronzes, ivory statues, porcelain, prints,
lace, sports memorabilia, Asian antiquities and a range of jewellery and decorative arts.

HICKMET FINE ARTS
75 Portobello Road, W11 * 0134 284 1508 *
www.hickmet.com * Mon–Fri 10:30–16:30, Sat 08:00–17:00

A lot of handsome, well-selected stock here, all neatly displayed. Much of it is small
in size; for instance, 19th- and early 20th-century (1840-1940) statuettes and animal sculptures by well known artists. A collection of lissom Erté enamelled bronze
figures dates later, but there are Art Déco pieces, glassware and vases by such artists
as Gallé and Witwe, mostly of the Belle Epoque period. 'A safe investment for the
future that can be enjoyed in the present' says Mr Hickmet. He also stocks 20th-cen-
tury furniture, from three-piece suites to coffee tables.

HUMBLEYARD FINE ART
141-149 Portobello Road, W11 * 01362 637793 *
Sat 06:00–14:00

Offerings here are largely nautical in nature, and include medical and marine items,
sailors' woolworks and shell valentines, as well as primitive pictures, needleworks,
boxes, pottery and general curiosities.

OLD FATHER TIME CLOCK CENTRE
Portobello Studios, 1st Floor, 101 Portobello Road, W11 *
www.oldfathertime.net * **Fri 11:00 — 14:00, Sat 08:00 — 14:00,**
other times by appointment

Full of quirky, eccentric timepieces, this is the place to come for virtually any kind of clock. They sell everything from mystery to skeleton clocks, and from eight-bell to mantle clocks.

REZAI ANTIQUE PERSIAN CARPETS
123 Portobello Road, W11 * **020 7221 5012** * **Mon–Fri**
10:00 — 17:00, Sat 06:00 — 18:00

A wide range of beautiful wool carpets, with some silk examples, too. Cushions and rugs are also sold, all in soft, vibrant colours and contrasts. They are spread out on show in this small space, and are also displayed on the walls and racks. There are many samples to look at here, from classic traditional Persian patterns to freestyle squares, with their modern, lively feel. Antique tapestries from Iran are sold as well.

WORLD FAMOUS PORTOBELLO MARKET
177 Portobello Road, W11 * **020 7436 9416** *
www.portobello-collections.co.uk * **Sat 05:30 — 17:30**

This large arcade has over 60 dealers, many of whom cater for tourists. Here you'll find mostly works of art, including British and European 20th-century works on paper, along with sculpture, contemporary still-life paintings and prints. Fair prices.

Tribal Gathering London

1 Westbourne Grove Mews, W11 *
www.tribalgatheringlondon.com * **Tube: Ladbroke Grove or**
Notting Hill Gate; Bus: 7, 12, 23, 27, 28, 31 * **Mon–Sat**
10:30 — 18:30

Antique shop: antique native arts, tribal pieces

A remarkably fine collection of worldwide antique native arts here, and quite a surprise to find it on a hidden side street beside Westbourne Grove, seemingly miles from the noise of the Portobello Market. The owner is a dedicated hunter of the rare and often elegant tribal pieces he shows. Most are old and polished with use, often with a sculptural feeling of considerable beauty.

Paddington and Bayswater

Noted for its grand railway station, first opened in 1854, Paddington lies near the Grand Junction Canal, which was recently developed into a smart living area. One notable resident of the area was Alexander Fleming, the scientist who discovered penicillin. As is true of much of London, Bayswater boasts a diverse mix of cultures and nationalities. The Bayswater Road, the main artery of the area, is lined mostly with hotels, office buildings and flats. There are a few antique shops worth visiting, though – if you know where to look.

Sean Arnold Sporting Antiques

21-22 Chepstow Corner, W2 * 020 7221 2267 *
Tube: Queensway, Notting Hill Gate; Bus: 7, 28, 31 *
Mon–Sat 10:00 – 18:00

Antique shop: sporting items: golf clubs, football articles, tennis racquets

A place for specialists – and for those seeking oddities. The many sporting items for sale in this large, crowded shop, established over 25 years ago, range from old golf clubs (as far back as 1840, when the game was invented in Scotland) to the occasional football articles – even to vintage luggage, globes and billiard tables. Tennis racquets go from a very affordable £10. There is also a mail-order service.

David Black Carpets

27 Chepstow Corner, W2 * 020 7227 2566 * www.david-black.com * Tube: Queensway, Notting Hill Gate; Bus: 7, 28, 31 * Mon–Sat 11:00 – 18:00

Large store: modern, custom-made carpets, a few antiques

Not too many antique rugs here, as most are modern and custom-made, and often outsize. There are a few antiques on offer, however – notably kilims, silk carpets, dhurries, and some of the wool carpets. Otherwise there's an interesting array of stock in this extensive store. Valuations made, along with restorations and a cleaning service.

Craven Gallery

30 Craven Terrace, W2 * **020 7402 2802** * **Tube: Lancaster Gate; Bus: 94, 148, 390** * **Mon–Fri 11:00—18:00, Sat 15:00—19:00, or by appointment**

Large store: 19th- and early 20th-century furniture, silver, glass, china

Established over 30 years ago, this large establishment, with a warehouse just off the Bayswater Road, offers a big stock of furniture, mostly from the 19th and early 20th centuries. There is also plenty of good silver and plate, as well as fine glass and china items from the same era.

Claire Guest Ltd

30a Queensway, W2 * **020 7243 1423** * **Tube: Bayswater; Bus: 94, 70, 148** * **Mon–Sat 09:30—17:00**

Mixed store: modern wares, antiques, second-hand items

Although this ordinary-looking store is classified as being for gifts, novelties and souvenirs, and is sub-titled 'giftware retailer', don't be put off, because there is a good mix of antique things hidden away amongst the modern stuff. There is also a section dedicated to 'second-hand goods', which can reveal some treasures as you rummage through.

The Mark Gallery

9 Porchester Place, W2 * **020 7262 4906** * **www.markgallery.co.uk** * **Tube: Marble Arch; Bus: 94, 148, 274** * **Mon–Fri 10:00—13:00, Sat 11:00—13:00**

Gallery: 16th- to 19th-century icons, modern drawings, prints, graphics

This long-established gallery is both inviting and airy. Mr Mark makes a speciality of Russian icons, mostly of the 16th to 19th centuries. There are also many drawings, prints and general graphics of the modern French school on show. Valuation and restoration services.

Putney

Approached by a wide bridge from the north bank of the Thames, this 19th-century riverside suburb has much to commend it, historically and otherwise. It was in the church of St Mary that Oliver Cromwell discussed his new Puritan republic after King Charles' execution for treason in 1649. Putney Bridge was built in 1882, and it is from here that the annual Oxford and Cambridge boat race departs. Putney's grand parade, the Embankment, houses many boating clubs and boat-houses, as well as some charming pubs and shops.

The Clock Clinic Ltd

85 Lower Richmond Road, SW15 * 020 8788 1407 * www.clockclinic.co.uk * Tube: East Putney; Bus: 22, 265, 485 * Tues–Fri 09:00 – 18:00, Sat 09:00 – 13:00

Antique shop: antique 'grandfather' clocks, barometers, watches

This small street-side shop is a welcoming place. A wide range of antique clocks tick away here, and a speciality is longcase clocks, also known as 'grandfather' clocks. The handsome specimens for sale here date from as early as the 17th century, going up to the late 19th. Antique barometers and some watches are also on sale. As the name of the shop suggests, repairs and restorations, from cases to dials, are carried out, most of the work being done right on the premises.

Hanshan Tang Books

Ashburton Centre, 276 Cortis Road, SW15 * 020 8788 4464 * www.hanshan.com * Mainline rail: Putney; Bus: 85, 170, 493 * By appointment only

Bookshop: second-hand Oriental books and publications

This is a specialist bookshop, concentrating on second-hand Oriental publications. These are mostly Chinese and Japanese, but there are also some from Korea and some central Asian countries. New books and magazines are also on sale. Regular catalogues, both general and specialist, are published. The firm will source special needs.

Richmond

A western suburb just beyond Kew Gardens with a distinct and quaint character of its own, Richmond is an old and charming London 'village', with many 17th- and 18th-century domestic brick buildings clustered around the large, open green and the venerable church. There is a River Thames frontage here, traversed by the famous Richmond Bridge, the oldest Thames bridge in Greater London. A tight net of streets and narrow lanes provides a vital centre for all kinds of local shopping, with branches of most major London department stores, bookshops and supermarkets all bunched together alongside pubs, cafés and shops of all kinds.

AZ Persian Carpet Gallery

1 Paved Court, The Green, TW9 * 020 8940 4435 * www.az-persiancarpets.com * Tube: Richmond; Bus: 65, 371 * Mon–Sat 10:00–17:00

Gallery: rugs, carpets, decorative boxes, Persian bibelots

A small shop, yet with lots to show. Its wide window on the court bulges with all sorts of rugs, carpets and cushions. Rugs range from small prayer rugs to larger Tabriz and Esfahan carpets, all from Iran. Inside on the ground floor, carpets are suspended all around the walls to show their full faces, and are also draped; yet others cover the floor, and there are more to be seen on the first floor. Also on sale are decorative old boxes and a selection of Persian bibelots. Cleaning, repair and valuation services available.

N. Courlander Ltd

55 George Street, TW9 * 020 8940 1645 * Tube: Richmond; Bus: 65, 371 * Mon–Sat 09:30–17:30

Jeweller's shop: mostly modern stock, but in classic styles

A grand, old-fashioned jeweller's shop – note the fine engraved plate-glass entry door. Windows extend around the corner and down the lane, indicating in gilded letters 'china, goldsmith and silversmith'. Each window shows a different aspect of the stock in hand, which is mostly modern, but in classic styles. The usual necklets, pendants, bangles and charms are sold, but the wide range here goes from small items of silver to salvers, scent bottles, boxed napkin rings and silver-mounted badger bristle brushes. Silver-framed mantel clocks and Moorcroft pottery are also sold.

Gregory and Co. Jewellers

15-17 Paved Court, TW9 ✳ **020 8332 6217** ✳
www.gregoryonline.co.uk ✳ **Tube: Richmond; Bus: 65, 371** ✳
Mon–Fri 10:30 — 17:00, Sat 10:00 — 18:00

Jewellery shop: mostly modern stock; antique gem repair service

On one of Richmond's many pleasant pedestrian lanes, just off the Green, this handsome shop has been established for over 15 years. With its 'British racing green' and gold façade and blinds, it offers a mostly modern yet well selected stock for investments in 'antiques of the future'. The owner will make and design pieces of jewellery at your request, and offers a repair service for antique gems.

Horton

2 Paved Court, TW9 ✳ **020 8332 1775** ✳ **Tube: Richmond;**
Bus: 65, 371 ✳ **Mon–Sat 09:00 — 17:00**

Shop: mostly modern stock, brooches, pins, necklaces

Marked with a swinging sign and the name in gilded capitals, a smart grey marble surround and entry pavement divides a rather severe and formal black and gold façade in half. Black blinds hood its two handsome show windows, containing a host of items. There are many brooches, pins and necklaces, mostly modern, but there are also some elegant Georg Jensen designs and numerous silver frames for photographs.

W. & A. Houben

2 Church Court, SW9 ✳ **020 8940 1055** ✳ **e-mail:**
ChrisDunlop1@aol.com ✳ **Tube: Richmond; Bus: 65, 371** ✳
Mon–Sat 10:00 — 18:00

Large shop: Second-hand books and first editions; some prints

W. & A. Houben is a comfortable bookshop where browsers are welcomed.

This double shop stands on a quiet paved court leading to the churchyard, now a pretty garden. It is a good source for a big stock of books on a multitude of subjects. There are two levels and a basement housing a warren of white painted rooms containing many second-hand volumes. Chairs are handily supplied for browsers. The owners also specialize in first editions. Some prints are on offer, too.

While you're in the area...
HAM HOUSE

Ham Street, Ham, Richmond-upon-Thames, TW10 * 020 8940 1950 * www.nationaltrust.org.uk * Mailine rail: Twickenham; Bus: 33, R70, R68, H22 * Mar–Oct: Mon–Wed, Sat & Sun 13:00 – 17:00 * Admission fee

A palatial house of the 17th century, and a rare revival of a royal style – that of Charles II and his wife, Queen Catherine of Braganza, who had apartments here. For admirers of the 17th century, this house is a repository of furnishings and decorations, with pieces remaining here from 1670, when Ham House was enlarged and furnished in Restoration style, which it still retains. The property is now run by the National Trust.

Wandsworth

Once famous for its hat industry, developed by its Huguenot residents in the 17th century, this residential and commercial suburb is contained within a large sprawl that is home to a major brewery (Young's Brewery) and a grim jail. Its name comes from the Wandle River, which debouches here. A great deal of traffic whizzes through the area, and big roads knife into it, though there is a nice, quiet common. Shops here tend to be specialist, and there are some good restoration services.

Edwardian Fireplace Co.

Former All Saints Church, Armoury Way, SW18 * **020 8870 0167** * **www.edwardianfires.com** * **Mainline rail: Wandsworth Town; Bus: 37, 170, 337** * **Mon–Sat 09:00 – 17:00**

Former church: *traditional, period and contemporary fireplaces*

The restored All Saints Church now accommodates this shop, in which you will find an extensive range of fireplaces and surrounds on three floors. Describing itself as 'a world of traditional, period and contemporary fireplaces', the shop stocks a wide range of original and antique surrounds and inserts, and accessories and tools as well.

Just a Second

284 Merton Road, SW18 * **020 8874 2520** * **Tube: Southfields; Bus: 39, 156** * **Tues–Sun 09:00 – 17:30**

Antique shop: *late 19th-century and early 20th-century furniture, silverware, mirrors; reproductions*

You will want to stay here for more than 'just a second'. Established for over 25 years, Mr Ferguson's roomy, atmospheric shop offers a delightful clutter of objects, mostly late 19th- and early 20th-century articles, from Victorian furniture to a great many interesting and unusual objects, including a selection of silverware and mirrors. Reproduction furniture too, and bric-à-brac; and there's also a restoration and valuation service.

Lloyds International Auction Galleries Ltd

Lloyds House, 9 Lydden Road, SW18 * 020 8788 7777 * www.lloyds-auction.co.uk * Mainline rail: Earlsfield; Bus: 44, 156, 270 * Collection and auction assessment Mon–Fri 08:30–17:00; auctions held every other Sat

Auction house: antique and modern furniture, pictures, prints, ceramics, silver, objets d'art, china, glassware, pictures and other collectables

Fortnightly Saturday sales of antique and modern furniture, pictures, prints, ceramics, silver, objets d'art, china, glassware, pictures and other collectables. The catalogue can be viewed on the website, or you can order it for delivery to your home.

Thornhill Galleries

319 Osiers Road, SW18 * 020 8874 2101 * www.thornhill-galleries.co.uk * Mainline rail: Wandsworth Town; Bus: 220, 270, 485 * Mon–Fri 09:00–17:15, Sat 10:00–12:00

Galleries: decorative and antique wooden effects, architectural articles

This is a centuries-old service for those seeking decorative and antique wooden effects, carvings and panelling. The specialities here include 17th- to 19th-century chimney pieces in wood, stone and marble, as well as antique grates, fenders and accoutrements. Valuation service and restoration of architectural items.

Services

Carvers and Gilders
Charterhouse Works, Eltringham Street, SW18 * 020 8870 7047 * www.carversandgilders.com * Mainline rail: Wandsworth Town; Bus: 44, 295, C3 * By appointment only

This shop offers a repair and restoration service, as well as a carving and gilding service.

Wimbledon

While the name of this area is known around the world for the annual lawn tennis championships that take place for a fortnight in early summer, there's much more to this spacious residential suburb. Take a stroll along The Broadway, full of shops and restaurants, or meander through the famous Common. Until its commercial centre was taken over by big companies, this large suburb used to have a good supply of antique shops clustered along its main street. Sadly, this is not so any more, and few remain today.

Cobb Antiques (Mark J West)

39b High Street, Wimbledon Village, SW19 * 020 8946 2811 * Mainline rail: Wimbledon; Bus: 93 * Mon–Sat 10:00 – 17:30

Antique shop: period glass

The English turned out millions of pieces of glass for the table in the 18th century as methods were perfected and glass became elegant and finely made, phasing out earlier metal containers such as tankards. There is some very fine period glass in this shop, and it's obviously a passion for Mark West: his card shows a superb frosted and patterned drinking glass with a painted poppy, emphasizing the high style of his stock. The range of glassware, from stemware and decanters to bowls and jugs, is wide, dating from 1700 right up to the Art Déco examples of the 1930s, with contemporary pieces in his collection, too.

Merton Abbey Mills Market

Watermill Way, off Merantun Way, SW19 * 020 8543 9608 * www.merton.gov.uk * Tube: South Wimbledon; Bus: 200, 470 * Sat & Sun 10:00–17:00

Market: assorted antiques, knick-knacks and handmade furniture

Occupying a tranquil spot by the River Wandle (albeit encircled by industrial estates and a Sainsbury's Savacentre), Merton Abbey Mills is chock full of arts and crafts, antiques, knick-knacks and handmade furniture. Weekly events consist of a collectors' market (Thursday 08:00–12:00), an antiques auction (Thursday mornings), and a toy collectors' fair (phone for details). And because the site used to be a silk printing works, there is also a museum dedicated to the mill as it was during the 19th century.

W. F. Turk

355 Kingston Road, Wimbledon Chase SW20 * 020 8543 3131 * www.wfturk.com * Mainline rail: Wimbledon Chase; Bus: 152, 163, 164 * Tues–Sat 09:00—17:30 (Sat closure at 16:00)

Large showroom: good-quality antique clocks

This shop claims to offer one of the largest selections of good-quality antique clocks in London. The showroom is literally crowded with examples, many handsome and distinguished ones going back to the William and Mary period, with an especially good representation of mantel and carriage clocks. There is also a timepiece repair and restoration service.

Services

Antiques of Wimbledon
329 Kingston Road, SW20 * 020 8540 7669 * www.antiquesofwimbledon.com * Mainline rail: Wimbledon Chase; Bus: 152, 163, 164 * Mon–Sat 09:00—18:00

This shop wears many hats, so to speak, as it is a buyer and dealer of antiques, collectables and second-hand furniture; it also undertakes house clearances. The owners seek all types of wares, including furniture, jewellery, clocks, barometers, scientific equipment, militaria, china, porcelain, glass, figures, flatware, old toys, curios, carpets, musical instruments, Oriental art, and even slot machines, pinball machines and classic British motorcycles. Fair prices are given, often in cash.

*Longcase clocks at W. F. Turk are of exceptional quality, and many
have lovely and unique decorative features.*

Day Trips

If you have a whole day to spare, try making an out-of-town visit
to one of the small country towns that still have a cluster of
antique shops and, sometimes, small markets. You will also see
some superb scenery, and perhaps eat at a village pub, or have a
picnic at a famously beautiful spot. (National Trust and English
Heritage annual guides are very useful for finding such sites.) In
some areas you may need to hop from town centre to town centre
to find antiques for sale, though some of the larger towns, such as
Bath, may have concentrations of antique outlets. Many of the
towns also have the lure of being historic centres and, in general,
are easily walked around. Check that the day you choose to visit is
not the local half-day closing, when all shops are shut after 13:00.

Practical Information for Day Trips

If you plan on travelling by train, you can pick up schedules and other information from any London rail station, or check the particular service provider.
If you wish to travel by bus, there are several firms offering services; at the time
of writing, the best in my opinion is the coach service National Express (from
the central Victoria Coach Station in London), which covers the whole country and has express non-stop services to many cities and towns. Along with
other operators, National Express offers frequent, fast service to centres such
as Oxford, Cambridge, Norwich, Brighton, Bath and Bristol. You can book
your National Express tickets online (and save the booking fee) at
www.nationalexpress.com, or call 08705 808080.

Alternatively, you might choose to travel by car. As anywhere, you can rent
a car by the day or by the week, or you may consider driver-guide services. Car
travel is advantageous in that it allows you to take in several town centres in one
day, as some towns may only have one or two antique shops. Local tourist
offices will have details.

The Cotswolds, Gloucestershire and Oxfordshire

Gloucestershire and Oxfordshire are charming, verdant counties, and both are popular tourist destinations. There are many fine sights in these regions, both natural and man-made, notably the thatched cottages of the west Cotswolds. The Cotswolds are home to one of the largest concentrations of art and antique dealers in the UK outside of London.

Architectural Heritage

Taddington Manor, Nr Cheltenham, GL54 5RY * 01386 584414 * www.architectural-heritage.co.uk * Mon–Fri 09:30–17:30, Sat 10:30–16:30

Antique shop: antique garden ornaments, chimney pieces, wood panelling

A family-run business selling an extensive collection of garden ornaments, along with some architectural antiques.

Cotswold Galleries

The Square, Stow-on-the-Wold, GL54 1AB * 01451 870567 * www.cotswoldgalleries.com * Mon–Sat 09:00–17:30

Gallery: traditional 19th- and 20th-century oil paintings and watercolours

A spacious and welcoming gallery offering an extensive selection of traditional fine original oil paintings and watercolours, mostly landscapes, by 19th- and 20th-century professional artists. Restorations of oils and watercolours are done here as well. Worldwide shipping available.

Duncan Baggott Antiques

Woolcomber House, Sheep Street, Stow-on-the-Wold, GL54 1AA * 01451 830662 * www.baggottantiques.com * Mon–Sat 09:00–17:30

Antique shop: furniture, paintings, domestic metalware, fireplace accoutrements and ornaments

Located in a substantial town house, this shop offers a diverse, extensive stock of fine English furniture, paintings, domestic metalware and fireplace accoutrements.

Fenwick & Fenwick

88-90 High Street, Broadway, WR12 7AJ * 01386 853227 * Mon–Sat 10:00 – 18:00, and by appointment

Antique shop: A wide selection of antiques, from furniture to accessories

This shop sells 17th-, 18th- and early 19th-century furniture in oak, mahogany and walnut. Also for sale are antique boxes, tea caddies, lace bobbins, corkscrews, early metalware, wood carvings, pewter, pottery and porcelain.

Greenway Antiques

90 Corn Street, Witney, OX8 7BU * 01993 705026 * www.greenwayantiques * Mon–Fri 09:30 – 17:30, Sat 10:00 – 16:00

Antique shop: furniture, brass and copper goods, fireplace accessories, garden furniture, decorative objects, unrestored rocking horses

An extensive shop comprised of three showrooms selling oak and mahogany furniture from the 17th to the early 20th centuries, brass and copper, pottery, fire tools, grates and fenders. Garden furniture is sold in season. Decorative objects and some lighting are also for sale. Unrestored rocking horses are a speciality.

The Old French Mirror Company

Unit 2, Hernes Estate, Henley-on-Thames, RG9 4NT * 01189 482444 * www.oldfrenchmirrors.com * By appointment only

Antique shop: gilded and painted old French mirrors

A lovely shop offering 19th- and early 20th-century gilded and painted French mirrors. The overmantels and trumeaux, and the pier glass, Venetian, oval and wall mirrors for sale here are sourced from various regions of France.

Hertfordshire

North of London and fringing the sprawl of the city, Hertfordshire is one of the 'home counties' and, of course, a home for many commuters. Many of its pretty villages make for lucrative antique hunting. Hemel Hempstead, famous for its 'magic' roundabout, holds an antique market every Wednesday. The saxon town of Hertford, site of an ancient castle, has many small antique shops stocked with all manner of items. The market in the town of Hitchin plays host to an antique market every Friday.

Beckwith & Son

St Nicholas Hall, St Andrew Street, Hertford, SG14 1HZ * **01992 582079** * **www.beckwithantiques.co.uk** * **Mon–Sat 09:00–17:30**

Multiple showrooms: comprehensive range of furniture, silver, glass, brass, copper, pewter, pictures, china, memorabilia

Housed in a Tudor-jettied half-timbered building together with the adjoining Victoria Hall, this antiques giant boasts nine showrooms filled with antique items, including furniture, silver, glass, brass, copper, pewter, pictures and china.

Bushwood Antiques

Stags' End Equestrian Centre, Gaddesden Lane, Redbourn, near Hemel Hempstead, HP2 6HN * **01582 794 700** * **www.bushwood.co.uk** * **Mon–Fri 08:30–16:00, Sat 10:00–16:00, or by appointment**

Antique warehouse: European furniture, period accessories

Plan a day or half-day outing for this very large warehouse-style outlet with a comprehensive stock of antiques and allied articles in its 15,000 square feet of space. English and European furniture is mostly on show, but there are also many period accessories and decorative items. Established over 30 years ago, this unusual showroom is about 20 miles from central London.

Sandgate, Nr. Folkestone, Kent

Despite the fact that Kent is the entry to cross-Channel ferries and the Tunnel, with a stop for Eurostar at Ashford International, it is still the Garden of England at heart, especially in the eastern part beyond Maidstone, the ancient capital city. Antique shops are scattered across East Kent, but there is a notable concentration of them along the High Street of the seaside settlement of Sandgate, near Folkestone, with shops situated close together alongside the beach. Regular antique fairs are held at the Grand Hotel, Folkestone Leas, every first Sunday in the month.

Christopher Buck Antiques

56-60 Sandgate High Street, Sandgate, CT20 3AP *
01303 221229 * **E-mail: cb@christopherbuck.co.uk** *
Mon-Sat (closed Wednesday) 10:00—17:00

Antique shop: 18th-century furniture, wine coolers, butlers' trays, silver

The setting here is ideal for the fine 18th-century furniture on show in this elegant shop with its Georgian-style interior. There are sets of dining chairs, sideboards, bookcases and desks, along with some fine Regency pieces. Some unusual articles too, such as wine coolers, butlers' trays and fine silver, with pieces of all sizes for sale.

Michael Fitch Antiques

95-99 Sandgate High Street, Sandgate, CT20 3BY *
01303 2491600 * **www.michaelfitchantiques.co.uk** *
Mon—Sat 10:00—17:00

Antique shop: Georgian furniture, clocks, mirrors, lamps, pictures, Oriental rugs

This is a spacious shop selling good Georgian furniture, clocks, mirrors, desks and impressive 19th-century bookcases. There are also Edwardian display cases, pairs of leather upholstered chairs and charming side tables, as well as lamps made from porcelain vases. Pictures and Oriental rugs are for sale as well.

Emporium Antiques

31-33 Sandgate High Street, Sandgate, CT20 3AH ⁂ **0130 3244430** ⁂ **Mon–Sat 10:00 – 17:00**

Antique shop: 19th-century to Edwardian furniture, also pieces by Frank Lloyd Wright and Stickley Brothers

A fascinating shop, neat and light, offering furniture and decorative pieces from the late 19th century to the Edwardian. Examples in wood, rattan and metalwork are for sale. Many items are specifically Gothic Revival, but other styles of the period are also represented. The genial owner likes to acquire American furniture by Frank Lloyd Wright and the Stickley Brothers of Chicago 'when I can get prime pieces'.

Freeman and Lloyd Antiques

44 Sandgate High Street, Sandgate, CT20 3AP ⁂ **01303 245 986** ⁂ **www.freemanandlloyd.com** ⁂ **Thurs–Sat 10:00 – 17:30, Mon & Wed by appointment**

Antique shop: Georgian and French furniture; porcelains, pictures

Within this long and narrow shop, with its single white-framed bay window, you'll find an array of goods, mostly Georgian pieces set against turquoise and green wallpaper. The elegantly arched showroom is in quiet good taste, and is a fine setting for the Hepplewhite chairs, break-fronts, candelabra and dining tables on display, with gold-framed pictures and mirrors on the walls. Porcelains, classical metal urns and inkstands are also sold, along with some French furniture.

Norden's

43 Sandgate High Street, Sandgate, CT20 3AH ⁂ **01303 248 477** ⁂ **Mon–Sat 09:00 – 17:00**

Antique shop: furniture, oil paintings, porcelain, silver, glassware

The nicely framed windows of this shop are well-dressed with samples of its stock, and the blue door opens to an interior with lots of fine furniture and oil paintings. Moss-green draperies make attractive backdrops for the good period pieces of the 18th and 19th centuries and the porcelain cups, plates and silver are for sale. There is an accent on fine glass here, with sets of wine glasses, decanters and pitchers. Unusual items include plant pedestals and busts.

Old English Oak and Old English Pine

100-102 Sandgate High Street, Sandgate, CT20 3BY *
01303 248560 * **Mon–Sat 10:00 – 18:00**

Two antique shops: furniture, garden furnishings, chandeliers, bird cages, wrought iron, ship models, dinner services, pottery

The names of these two shops, sitting side by side and with a mutual owner, describe what is on offer, but there is much more in these large, crowded spaces with their blue-tiled floors. There are masses of things to look at here: chandeliers, bird cages, wrought iron items, ship models and dinner services; also lots of pottery. Some pieces are big and Victorian. There is also a conservatory, displaying casual and garden furnishings, at the back. Very helpful owner.

Sandgate Passage

82 Sandgate High Street, Sandgate, CT20 3AH *
01303 850 973 * **Tues–Sat 10:30 – 16:00, closed lunchtimes**

Covered passage: books, prints, posters

This is indeed an old, winding covered passage with a narrow street frontage, but it is stuffed to the gills with things — mostly paper items. Walls display old posters, though the stock is largely second-hand books and old prints, but there are also unusual items, such as collections of cigarette cards, postcards, discs and photographs. In the back room are paperback books and pamphlets, as well as various local interest publications.

Bath, Somerset

Somerset is said to be one of the most beautiful counties in Britain. Claimed as the 'home' of the legendary King Arthur, and the birthplace of Christianity in England, today it is a popular place to visit for everything from its ancient burial grounds to its lovely villages. One place of note is the city of Bath, with its Roman baths, Saxon Abbey and Georgian terraces, squares and crescents. Bath also has a thriving and varied circuit of antique shops. Look for a useful folder on shops and services in the area, supplied by the Bath & Bradford On Avon Antique Dealers Association. There is also an annual antique dealers' fair in March; check the Association's website for details: www.babaada.com.

Kit Alderson

The Old Rectory, Vicarage Lane, Compton Dando, BS39 4LA
❋ **01761 490137** ❋ **e-mail: kit.alderson@btopenworld.com** ❋
Mon–Sun 10:00 – 18:00, appointment suggested

Antique shop: English 18th-century furniture

Compton Dando is a village between Bristol and Bath, and here off the A39 road you will find this pleasing country shop. Kit Alderson likes the unusual in English 18th-century antiques, so his is a carefully chosen specialist range. Georgian tables, chairs, chests, desks and associated items of the same period are sold.

The Antiques Warehouse

57 Walcot Street, Bath, BA1 5BN ❋ **01225 444 201** ❋
Mon–Sat 10:00 – 17:30

Antique warehouse: 18th- and 19th-century furniture

When driving out of Bath along the London Road to look at the antique shops on the way to Bradford on Avon, take Walcot Street and look for this large outlet. On two spacious floors you will find a mass of good 18th- and 19th-century furniture and associated wares, especially tables and chairs, with a special interest in chests and wardrobes. Delivery service available.

Mary Cruz Antiques

5 Broad Street, Bath, BA1 5LJ * **01225 334 174** *
Mon–Sat 10:00 – 18:00

Antique shop: 18th- and 19th-century English and European furniture

On Broad Street, which leads to Lansdown Road (a scenic way to enter Bath from the north), this shop, specializes in fine quality English and European furniture of the 18th and 19th centuries, with a constant stock of decorative items of the period, too. Unusually, there's also a sculpture aspect here, with a number of stone and bronze pieces on show. Oil paintings and Latin and western American art are for sale as well.

Frank Dux Antiques

33 Belvedere, Bath, BA1 5HR * **01225 312 367** *
www.antique-glass.co.uk * **Tues–Sat 10:00 – 18:00**

Antique shop: glassware

For collectors of old glass, this is a little treasure of a shop – the specialities are 18th-century drinking glasses, from rummer to elegant wine glass. There's also a range of decanters and later Victorian tableware and glass. They stock 'anything eye-catching', sometimes running to the exotic and extraordinary, such as Venetian Murano glassware.

E. P. Mallory & Son Ltd

1-4 Bridge Street, Bath, BA2 4AP * **01225 442 210** *
www.mallory-jewellers.com * **Mon–Sat 09:30 – 17:15**

Antique shop: gems, jewellery, silver items

A long-established jeweller's in the very centre of the city, situated on the corner of the High Street and just beside the famous Pulteney Bridge. The large stock within this small, atmospheric shop encompasses antique and second-hand gems, as well as modern jewellery. Small silver items and Sheffield plate are also for sale, along with some unusual pieces, including snuff boxes and general curiosities.

James Townsend Antiques

1 Saville Row, Alfred Street, Bath, BA1 2QP * **01225 332 290**
* **www.jtownsendantiques.co.uk** * **Mon–Sat 10:00–17:00**

Antique shop: 'an eclectic mix' of items, including furniture, china, unusual decorative items and clocks

Take a trip up the hill to the top of the town and you'll find this large corner shop, with its high ceilings and items for sale spilling out on to the pavement. The owner describes his stock as 'an eclectic mix', and it is indeed, with a fascinating array of goods displayed in its four large rooms. Specialities include furniture, china, unusual decorative items and clocks.

Walcot Reclamation

108 Walcot Street, Bath, BA1 5BG * **01225 448 163** *
www.walcot.com * **Mon–Sat 09:00–17:00**

Antique yard: architectural items, reproduction shop

Near the Antiques Warehouse, on the other side of the street, this is a very worth-while place to visit. An old builder's yard has been used to house the many architectural antiquities on show in this large space. The site specializes in chimney pieces, fireplaces, panelling, doors, wrought iron, bathroom fittings and brassware. Rick Knapp also offers a restoration service in his workshop, and the Repro Shop, situated within Walcot Yard, provides high-quality replicas of fixtures and fittings rarely available in sufficient quantity from salvage. Mail order available.

Woodbridge and Bungay, Suffolk

Suffolk is a lovely country, deeply rural and edged by the North Sea along its Eastern shore, where it runs up to neighbouring Norfolk. Away from the main roads, this is definitely farm country, with lovely old market towns and villages with huge churches. Suffolk has many literary and artistic associations. You can view the beauty of painter John Constable's country in the South, visit Bury St Edmund's venerable theatre or go to the Music Festival at Aldeburgh, founded by the composer Benjamin Britten. Two particularly prolific antique-hunting towns are Woodbridge and Bungay; if you rise early, you can easily visit both in a single day.

Woodbridge

An ancient, compact town, ranged up- and downhill with handsome old streets, this is a lively shopping centre. The antique establishments form a tight circuit here, and there is a range of shops of varied interest to be found. Almost all of the shops are situated in atmospheric old buildings, some of which are unique. Go around the handsome old settlement, then venture up to the town square at the top of the town, with its 16th-century houses still intact. To one side of the square, steps descend down to give a glimpse of the stone-framed porch of the big, handsome old church in its churchyard.

Hamilton Antiques

**5 Church Street, Woodbridge, IP12 1DS * 01394 387 222 *
09:30 – 13:00, and 14:00 – 17:30; closed Wed and Sat**

Antique shop: Georgian and 19th-century furniture and furnishings

Here you'll find many Georgian and 19th-century pieces, from stools and clocks to large cabinets, desks, dressers and chests, with mirrors and candlesticks, too. Everything for sale is in very good working order, and is displayed with care in these spacious, well decorated premises. All pieces are well lit, too — no peering into dusty dark corners!

Anthony Hurst Antiques

13 Church Street, Woodbridge, IP12 1DS * 01394 382 500 * Mon–Fri 09:30 – 13:00, and 14:00 – 17:30, closed Wed and Sat

Antique shop: 18th- and 19th-century furniture and furnishings

Established since 1956, this is a handsomely designed place for good quality furniture of the 18th and 19th centuries, including imposing chests and elegant sofas. Set against soft blue walls are plenty of Georgian examples, from screens to side tables and stools, as well as sets of dining chairs, dining tables and desks. Mirrors are displayed, some in beautifully lacquered frames, along with silver salvers and trays.

Ray and Mary Lambert and Son

The Bull Ride, 70a New St, Woodbridge, IP12 1DX * 01394 382 380 * e-mail: mary@lambert667.fsnet.co.uk * Mon–Sat 10:00 – 13:00, and 14:00 – 17:00

Antique shop: 19th- and 20th-century furniture and furnishings

Plenty of furniture here, much of it unvarnished oak, but there is lots of good 'old brown', as well as polished and veneered pieces such as occasional and demi-lune tables, and a range of other useful pieces, from chairs and dining tables to corner cupboards. 'I get a wide cross-section of people', says the helpful owner, 'the young ones who can't afford to get into the top of the market, and the elderly looking for something handy'.

Edward Masson Clocks

8 Market Hill, Woodbridge, IP12 4LU * 01394 380 235 *
Mon–Sat 10:00 – 17:30, Wed 10:00 – 13:00

Antique shop: clocks and timepieces, repairs

Set against avocado-green walls in this atmospheric little establishment, a motley collection of timepieces and clock workings is scattered about this pleasant shop. There is a variety of styles and periods, including longcase and French examples. As well as selling clocks, repairs are carried out in a workshop on the premises: a list of repair charges is displayed in the window, along with photographs of other clocks in stock.

Sarah Meysey-Thompson Antiques

10 Church Street, Woodbridge, IP12 4LU * 01394 382144 *
Mon–Sat 10:30 – 16:00, or by appointment

Antique shop: glassware, repro articles, decorative items

A neat and charming shop situated halfway down the hill, with old-style, red-framed show windows and a tiled entrance. Neatly presented, there's a well chosen, wide-ranging antiques stock here, ranging from chandeliers to glassware, with some good wine glasses and period decanters, too, along with a selection of old tea-boxes and gilded items. Other wares include good quality decorative items and bibelots, metal and brassware urns and bowls, and fireplace tools and fenders. Prints in original wooden frames are also sold, along with some reproduction articles.

Isobel Rhodes

10 & 12 Market Hill, Woodbridge, IP12 4LU *
01394 382763 * Mon–Sat 10:00 – 17:00

Two antique shops: 17th- and 18th-century furniture, furnishings

Off the narrow footpath bordering the handsome wide square you will find these two small shops, situated side by side. Within, 17th- and 18th-century furniture and other items are set out in a neat display. Wares for sale include chests and dining tables in mahogany and oak, sets of dining chairs, handsome place settings, small decorative items and antique rugs. There is also a good selection of candlesticks, brass coasters and pottery here.

A. G. Voss

24 Market Hill, Woodbridge, IP12 4LU * 01394 385830 *
By appointment only

Antique shop: rugs, period items, furniture, glass

This is the sort of place in which you might find a treasure. A large, long-established shop with a mass of stuff on display, from brass chandeliers to painted pottery pigs, entry requires you to tread upon old rugs thrown on the wooden floors, upon which is featured a mixture of Georgian, Edwardian and Victorian items. There is some good furniture here, especially chests of drawers, mirrors and chairs. Kitchen items include preserving pans and pottery. The owner likes old glass, and it shows: there are plenty of wine glasses, old bottles and decanters for sale here. Prints and framed items such as old playbills are also sold.

Woodbridge Gallery

23 Market Hill, Woodbridge, IP12 4LX * 01394 386500 *
Sat 10:00 – 17:30, at all other times by appointment

Gallery: pictures, lamps, silver articles

While you're in the area...
SUTTON HOO

Tranmer House, Sutton Hoo, Woodbridge, IP12 3DJ *
01394 389700 * www.nationaltrust.org.uk * Check
website or call for opening times * Small admission fee

One of the most important archaeological sites in Britain, Sutton Hoo is the burial ground of the Anglo-Saxon pagan kings of East Anglia. Archaeological digs have unearthed numerous and now famous treasures, many of which are on display in the museum, housed in a substantial Edwardian dwelling. The Sutton Hoo Estate includes the museum, 254 acres of grass heath, salting and woodland on the Deben estuary, and the burial grounds themselves.

Standing boldly at the head of the square is an impressive and handsome old house: its large show windows tell you at once that this is a gallery of pictures. Most of these are original 19th- and 20th-century works, but there are prints for sale as well. In addition there are antiquities – mostly Edwardian lamps and 19th century silver articles, including old silver picture frames. There is a framing service offered as well.

Services

Woodbridge Violins
26 Market Hill, Woodbridge, IP12 4LX * 01934 383 150 *
Mon–Sat 09:00 – 17:00

This venue is dedicated to the creation of new violins and the restoration of old ones. The makers and repairers of these stringed instruments sit at their benches in a small beamed studio at the front of an old house, its large window facing right onto the street. This is not a shop, but rather a workplace, and all the tools and aids to violin-making are on view. You can watch the artists working, carving, stringing and finishing the developing instruments. A rare and fascinating spectacle.

Bungay

This charming old market town is almost in Norfolk, for it is located in the extreme north-east of the county. Bungay is a tightly planned place, with a ruined nunnery beside its large, redundant church (worth a visit), and a round-towered Saxon church is close by. Easy to walk around, there is a good number of straightforward antique shops here, most of them located on Earsham and Broad streets. There is an ancient 12th-century four-towered castle to explore, too.

Black Dog Antiques

51 Earsham Street, Bungay, NR35 2PB * 01986 895554 *
Mon–Sat 09:00 – 17:00

Antique shop: general antiques, Saxon and Roman antiquities

This shop sells a wide range of goods, including furniture made from oak, mahogany and stripped pine, china, linen and collectables, with some Saxon and Roman antiquities sold as well.

Friend or Faux

28 Earsham Street, Bungay, NR35 1AQ * **01986 896170** *
Sat 10:00 — 17:30, other times by appointment

Antique shop: porcelain, lighting, Victorian watercolours

This wittily named shop has a carefully selected stock, carrying 19th-century porcelain, as well as lighting from the 1800s all the way to the 1950s. There are also some low-priced Victorian watercolours for sale.

Services

Earsham Hall Pine
Earsham Hall, Bungay, NR35 2AN * **01986 893 423** *
www.earshamhallpine.co.uk * **Mon — Sat 09:00 — 17:00,**
Sun 10:30 — 17:00

Situated just a little west of Bungay, this shop offers an unusual service — they will make specific pieces of furniture or panels to your own design using genuine antique pine wood recovered from old buildings. Or you can choose new wood from renewable plantations in Finland. In addition, there is a stock of old pine pieces from the UK and some Eastern European countries, and a range of hand-waxed modern pine furniture is also on show.

Farnham, Surrey

Long known as part of the 'Home Counties' – that is, those surrounding London – Surrey has splendid scenery, charming villages and cathedral towns to visit. Just an hour's drive from London lies Farnham, an old English market town with narrow streets, and lined with some of the finest Georgian architecture in the South of England. There is also a delightful parish church, and a castle dating back to the 12th century. There are a few antique centres and warehouses here, too, where hunters can spend a happy day browsing, making the town very much worth a day trip.

The Antiques Warehouse

Badshot Farm, St Georges Road, Runfold, Badshot Lea, Nr Farnham, GU9 9HY * 01252 317590 * Open all week 10:00 – 17:30

Antique warehouse: general antiques, collectables, jewellery, silverware, toys and garden ornaments

Housed in two spacious, picturesque converted Elizabethan tithe barns accommodating over 50 dealers of antiques, here you will find an abundance of collectables, jewellery, silverware, toys and garden ornaments.

The Packhouse

Hewett's Kilns, Tongham Road, Runfold, Farnham, GU10 1PJ * 01252 781010 * www.packhouse.com * Mon–Fri 10:30 – 17:30, Sat & Sun 10:00 – 17:30 *

Antique centre: general antiques, interiors accessories

This centre accommodates over 100 dealers in a 400-year-old hop kiln, offering an eclectic mix of antiques and interiors accessories. There is a vast array of furniture on offer, including pieces from England, France, Italy and the East. Home accessories such as mirrors, clocks, picture frames and ceramics are also for sale. There is a café on the premises. A UK home delivery and assembly service is offered.

Petworth, West Sussex

The ancient market town of Petworth has, in recent times, become widely renowned for its fascinating array of shops and galleries specializing in a diverse range of antiques and works of art. It is commonly recognized as the centre of the antique business in the South of England. Having been voted Best Antiques Town at the 2004 British Antiques & Collectables (BACA) awards, it is well worth a day trip by those seeking antiques. It is also home to Petworth House, where visitors can view a superb collection of art treasures set amidst a landscaped garden designed by Capability Brown.

Angel Antiques

Lombard St, GU28 0AG * 01798 343306 * www.angel-antiques.com * Mon–Sat 10:00 – 17:30, Sun by appointment

Antique shop: 17th-, 18th- and 19th-century English and French furniture, paintings, ceramics

The house in which this shop is located is in itself worth a visit. Dating back to 1543, it was built by a wealthy local squire; the old oak beams and inglenooks are still in place. Here you'll find 17th-, 18th- and 19th-century English and French furniture, paintings and ceramics, including a good deal of Ironstone.

Richard Gardener Antiques

Swan House, Market Square, GU28 OAN * 01798 343411 * www.richardgardnerantiques.co.uk * open every day 10:00 – 17:30

Antique shop: period furniture and art, porcelain, Staffordshire figurines, bronzes, silver, paintings, globes

This vast shop sells all manner of antiques, from butler's trays to champagne glasses, and from globes to 18th-century mirrors. The speciality is in Victorian Staffordshire figures, and the shop claims that it 'will always have one of the best selections available in the country'.

Muttonchop Manuscripts

The Playhouse Gallery, Lombard Street, GU28 0AG * 01798 344471 * www.mrmuttonchops.com * Wed–Sat 10:00 – 16:00

Antique shop: antique books, maps and prints

Owner Roger Clarke and his wife, Penny, are the only two staff members here, giving personal service to all of their customers. Book sold are primarily non-fiction, covering a range of subjects, including books on London, antiques reference and general antiquarian. Some fiction is also sold, such as classic sets of Dickens, Brontë and Defoe. Maps and prints are for sale here as well.

Petworth Antiques Centre

East Street, Petworth, GU28 OAB * 01798 342073 * www.petworthantiquecentre.co.uk * Mon–Sat 10:00 – 17:30

Antique centre: over 30 dealers selling a wide range of antiques

This antiques centre has over 30 dealers selling a vast selection of items. Specialities include English, Continental and Oriental furniture, garden ornaments, paintings, books, pottery, glass, tools, jewellery, textiles and rugs.

Nicholas Shaw Antiques

Virginia Cottage, Lombard Street, GU28 0AG * 01798 345146 * www.nicholas-shaw.com * Tues–Sat 10:00 – 17:30, Sun and Mon by appointment

Antique shop: fine and rare English, Scottish and Irish silver

This small shop specializes in a large variety of fine antique silver from the 16th to the 20th century, particularly rare collectors' items. There is a good selection of Scottish and Irish provincial silver here, too. They also undertake valuations and restorations.

Annual Fairs

London's principal annual fairs are always well attended, and usually carry an entry fee. However, a friendly dealer will often give a free invitation, especially to frequent customers. For up-to-date fair information and for details on selected antique fairs held throughout the UK, pick up a copy of *The Collector* magazine, distributed throughout antique shops and centres, hotels and other outlets in the UK. See also the BADA (British Antiques Dealers Association) website (www.bada.org) for details of fairs and events attended by its numerous members and friends.

The Grosvenor House Art & Antiques Fair

Grosvenor House Hotel, 80-90 Park Lane, W1 * 020 7399 8100 * www.grosvenor-antiquesfair.co.uk * Tube: Marble Arch, Hyde Park Corner; Bus: 9, 10, 94, 148 * Tickets sold in advance; prices are around £16 for a single, £27 for a double admission * Free handbook upon admission

One of the grandest of London occasions is the annual Grosvenor House Art & Antiques Fair held in this large London hotel, opposite Hyde Park on Park Lane. At the Fair, which occurs annually for nine days in early June, up to 100 international dealers have their wares on show, with articles for sale ranging in period from 3000 BC to the present. The Great Room usually houses the most elegant pieces of all, originating from all over the world, and on display in a series of show windows, immaculate stands and period rooms. Throughout the Fair's many rooms, top dealers offer for sale furniture, paintings, sculpture, Oriental works, silver, glass, porcelain, ceramics, bibelots, books, prints, textiles and jewellery. The range is extraordinarily wide, and it goes without saying, very expensive. Items on sale have all been vetted by experts. A fine sight, previewed in the well-illustrated accompanying handbooks, which are distributed from early May (call or check the website for details). There is a preview day and, framing the Fair, many social events, with a grand charity reception and dinner held at the hotel during the run.

The Olympia Fine Art & Antiques Fairs

The Olympia Exhibition Centre, Hammersmith Road, W14 * **0870 126725** * **www.olympia-antiques.com** * **Tube: Olympia; Bus: 9, 10, 27, 28, 49, 391** * **Ticket prices are around £10 for a pre-booked single, £16 at the door** * **Free guide upon admission**

This fair is always well-indicated, with large signs outside the building advertising this important event. The Fair, which lasts for about a week, is held every year in February, June and November, and the February event is usually the biggest. The Centre's lofty halls glitter with splendid pieces on two levels, so allow lots of time to wander around and enjoy this sociable occasion. It's a friendly event, with many dealers only too glad to talk about their displays, which range from simple counters displaying small objects to large, beautifully organized show rooms. Some dealers appear at every Fair, others only at specific ones. Popular and very busy, the Fairs attract a wide range of antique and art galleries from all over the world, though the accent is distinctly British. The assembled dealers tend to be very focused on what they offer, so stands can be quite specific in their interests. There are many picture and sculpture gallery presentations, too, as well as offices to help ship, insure and pack purchases. This is a good fair to visit if antique collecting is a new hobby or a possible vocation, as the quality is high and one can learn a lot.

The BADA Antiques & Fine Art Fair

Duke of York's Square, King's Road, Chelsea, SW3 * **020 7589 6108** * **www.bada-antiques-fair.co.uk** * **Tube: Sloane Square; Bus: 11, 19, 22, 49** * **Ticket prices are around £10 for a single, £15 for a double admission** * **Free guide upon admission**

The British Antique Dealers' Assocation's label is a very important one, and is seen only in top shops (when shopping, look for their blue and gold shield on members' shop doors). Held annually, usually in the second week of March, BADA's fair is a very important one for the top dealers and gallery owners in the UK (and also from abroad), and is a busy and sociable affair. Held in the one-time baronial barracks of the Duke of York's regiment at the top of the King's Road in Chelsea, this is a large and airy place, and a good location to see some of the finest furniture and bibelots from around the UK and beyond. There are lots of stands selling remarkable pieces of all periods, from Georgian furniture to Oriental ceramics, and from Old Master paintings to wonderful textiles and jewellery. There are around 100 exhibitors in total, all of whom are BADA members, and together they constitute the 'cream' of the UK's antiques industry.

The Decorative Antiques & Textiles Fair

Battersea Park, Chelsea Gate, SW11 ＊ 020 7624 5173 ＊ www.decorativefair.com ＊ Tube: Sloane Square; Bus: 137 ＊ During the Fair a free shuttle bus operates regularly from the marquee and the Moat House Hotel in Sloane Square ＊ Tickets sold at the door; prices are around £8 for a single ＊ Free catalogue upon admission

This week-long Fair is held in central London three times a year: in January, April and October. The year 2005 marked its twentieth anniversary. The Fair is held in a large marquee in London's leafy Battersea Park, which borders the Thames opposite Chelsea and is connected by Chelsea Bridge and also the Victorian arches of the grandiose Albert Bridge. The main entrance to the Fair is at Chelsea Gate off the Chelsea Bridge crossing. On display are the wares of around 100 dealers from all over the UK and Europe. Not all of the items for sale are antiques, however – the Fair also has fabric and interior decorator representation, and has recently extended its deadline to allow in original art and design-led, limited-edition interior accessories, including furniture, textiles, wallpaper, glass, porcelain and silverware.

The LAPADA Fairs

Venues vary; check www.lapada2.co.uk for up-to-date information

Like the British Antique Dealers' Association, The Association of Art and Antique Dealers (LAPADA), the largest association of professional art and antique dealers in the UK, adheres to a code of practice. Its symbol – a golden chandelier – can be found in shop windows and at fairs, and signifies to the public that it can buy from the accredited vendor with confidence. Every year, LAPADA stages one or two antique fairs, at which only members of LAPADA can exhibit. This means that all goods for sale at the fair will have been vetted by independent experts, so quality and authenticity are assured. A wide variety of goods is typically on sale, from antiquities to contemporary fine art.

Useful Information

Export duty and VAT

There are a few rules to follow if you plan on exporting your UK-bought goods abroad:

1) Any object worth more than £30,400 that is being exported to a location outside Europe will need an export license. This can typically be provided by the dealer, but if not, contact: **The Department for Culture, Media and Sport, Export Licensing Unit, 2-4 Cockspur Street, London SW1Y 5DH; 020 7211 6200.**

2) If you are shipping your purchases to the US, all wooden furniture is exempt from import duty. Antiques made from any other material must be 100 years old or older to be exempt from duty. Ask your dealer for an invoice that reflects the age of the piece.

3) Exports to Australia are charged a 10 per cent Goods & Services Tax (GST). Similarly, exports to Canada are charged a seven per cent GST if the intention is to re-sell them.

4) Most antique dealers are VAT-registered, and as such, they have to pay 17.5% VAT on any goods that they sell within the UK. However, if the goods are being sold for export, the dealer will not have to pay the VAT. Some dealers will give purchasers a discount on the goods to reflect this saving.

Insurance and Valuation

Not only will you need a good export service if you are sending antiques out of London, you will also need sound advice on insurance. This is, of course, a very difficult business, and depends on more than a simple basic valuation at current value – which many shops themselves offer as a service. Insurance needs expert advice. Furthermore, what sum you decide to insure for depends on a host of factors: current prices, rarity, fragility, age and condition of the article, what it's made of, even current events if the country or state you are exporting to is volatile. Again, the shop you purchase from can proffer advice, but there are also a number of individual specialists in antique and art valuations in London. Their advice may well be vital if exporting antiques, as well as for insurance purposes. Here are a few London-based companies offering valuation services.

The Antiques Warehouse

9-14 Deptford Broadway, SE8 4PA * 020 8691 3062 *
e-mail: martin@antiquewarehouse.co.uk

A worldwide valuation service to 'existing and potential' customers of the Antiques Warehouse. Experienced valuers here will endeavour to value and give an approximate age to your furniture and other items. Simply send a photograph of the item, by e-mail or by post, and whatever additional information you can provide. This service incurs an administrative charge of £10.

AON artscope/Needham Jobson

8 Devonshire Square, Cutlers Gardens, EC2 * 020 7882 0470 * www.aonartscope.com. Other location: 67-68 Jermyn Street, St James's, SW1 * 020 7839 8340

This firm is a specialist insurance broker for dealers, auctioneers, collectors and private clients. The focus here is on high-value assets and general valuables. The firm will tailor services to individual needs.

Bonhams

101 New Bond Street, W1 * 0207 447 7447 *
www.bonhams.com

One of the world's largest and oldest auction houses, Bonham's offers a network of experienced general valuators. Support and expertise is provided by its 40 specialist departments, and covers everything from the valuation of an Alfa Romeo to that of a Zograscope! Valuations are done for insurance purposes, as well as for auctions.

Christie's

85 Old Brompton Road, SW7 * 020 7930 6074 *
www.christies.com

The South Kensington salesroom offers a free valuation service. Bring your object or work of art to the valuation counter, and a specialist from the appropriate department will provide you with a valuation without any obligation to sell. You can bring in your item during business hours (see page 57), but a special appointment is recommended to ensure the availability of a specialist for your category.

Criterion Auctioneers

**53 Essex Road, Islington, N1 * 020 7359 5707 *
www.criterion-auctioneers.com**

The valuation team here gives free verbal appraisals at either the saleroom or over the telephone, from photographs or from e-mails. Written insurance and probate valuation is also available at one and a half per cent of the total value, with a minimum charge of £90.

Shipping the Goods

If shipping your newly purchased antiques to a destnation outside London, you'll want to use a specialist shipping and packing company that deals exclusively with art and antiques. These companies are used to shipping items that have special needs, ranging from insurance requirements to conservation. For example, some items may need to be kept in special conditions to prevent deterioration, and specialist companies can provide humidity-controlled warehouses, offering ideal conditions for delicate items while in storage. While most shops will know of a reliable shipping and packing company, and will likely take care of the matter for you, it is nevertheless useful to have some contacts of one's own. Below is a short list of specialist shipping and packing companies.

Anglo Pacific International

Unit 1, Bush Industrial Estate, Standard Road, North Acton, London, NW10 * 020 8965 0667 * www.anglopacific.co.uk

Specialist antique shippers serving destinations worldwide. Delivery of goods via sea, air or road. Clients include antique-dealers and bespoke furniture-makers.

Atlantic Fine Art and Antiques (Packing & Shipping) Ltd

Unit 23, Riverside Business Park, Lyon Road, Merton, London, SW19 * 020 8544 9919 *

Packing and shipping of antiques and fine arts by sea, air or road.

Clarks of Amersham

Higham Mead, Chesham, Buckinghamshire, HP5 2AH * 01494 774186 * www.clarksofamersham.com

Antiques and fine art carriers, offering a comprehensive specialist service to the antiques trade.

Davies Turner Worldwide Movers Ltd

49 Wates Way, Mitcham, CR4 4HR * 020 7622 4393 * E-mail: removals@daviestumer.co.uk

Expert packing and shipping worldwide by sea, air or road, to individual requirements. Offices throughout the US.

Locksons

29 Broomfield Street, London, E14 * 0207 7515 8600 * www.lockson.co.uk

International shippers, packers and removers of fine art and antiques. Insurance consultations available.

Top Hunting Tips

Here are a few tips on getting a head start on any fairs, shows, auctions and new openings about town:

* Magazine Subscriptions: For those looking for old prints and paintings, monthly London-based publication *The Collector* can be very useful. Issued free, it can be picked up at galleries throughout London. In it you'll find a listing of all the shows and ventures upcoming, along with handy maps of neighbourhoods and the specific locations of galleries.

* Area Guides: Some shopping areas, such as Portobello Road Market, publish individual shopping guides or handbooks for visitors to the area. These guides often list each shop and, helpfully, note its speciality. A map of the area is also usually provided. Ask for a copy when visiting local dealers.

* Mailing Lists: When visiting galleries and antique shops, ask if they have a mailing list. If you have a special interest, then you are of interest to them, and may benefit from new brochures and advance notices of exhibitions or of newly acquired objects suitable for your collection. This service is usually free. If you turn out be a buyer, then invitations to openings may well also result.

* Websites: Some antique shops and galleries display their wares on their websites, and many auction houses have their catalogues online. A quick perusal from the comfort of your office or home can cut out a lot of searching time and direct you to the venue that has exactly what you're looking for.

* Museum Reproduction Shops: If the object of your desire lies outside your financial reach, or if you just can't find it for sale anywhere, it is always worthwhile checking museum and gallery reproduction shops. The great museums and galleries in central London all have excellent examples of these shops – in fact, some people spend more time exploring them than the galleries themselves. Aside from books, postcards and print reproductions, there are often hosts of reproductions of the items in the collections themselves. These are almost always of the highest quality, as befits such organizations, and are as true to original subjects as possible – so true in fact that sometimes they seem absolutely identical. You can thus acquire a classic piece and, at the same time, assist in the gallery's funding.

Taking Care in London

Personal Safety

London is in general a very safe city, especially in the central areas. Don't be put off by warnings of danger – but at the same time, do take normal care. Keep valuables close, as pockets can get picked and bags do get snatched sometimes, especially in crowded places such as markets. If you run into trouble, contact the police at once, as many stolen items do get returned.

Stolen Goods

A little common sense and practicality avoids problems – but we have all heard of burglaries in which the times were brief between the actual theft and the re-appearance of goods, often within hours, at outlets such as street markets. Sometimes the goods may have changed hands several times before arriving at a stall, each intermediary transaction adding to the price, of course, in this quick progression. Possessing or selling stolen antiquities does present problems, as you will know from high-profile cases of very valuable items illegally sold.

It is not likely that you will run across purchase problems in London, but a few pointers are useful. The Metropolitan Police is always eager to track down robberies or chase stolen goods. They operate a special section, and their advice when buying or selling goods is to make as sure as you can that you are not buying anything suspicious, and that your contacts are professional. Obviously it is best only to deal with people who have an establishment, which means an address and a telephone number, and to have a receipt issued. In markets in particular, where the dealers deal from stalls and may only take cash, there is often a strong element of trust involved in any transaction.

Protecting your Goods from Theft

Obviously you should consider adequate insurance for your goods, and you should also make sure that you have a complete photographic record. To protect your goods it is helpful to keep a catalogue of them, with a close-up range of detailed photographs. Stolen items can often be recovered if you act swiftly to report any losses, and have photographs as well as descriptions.

Forbidden Exports

When buying anywhere abroad, always be wary of what you're purchasing. If you suspect, for whatever reason, that the article may have been stolen, or sent from a country where export is prohibited for various reasons, then simply don't buy it. Otherwise, a fine is likely and confiscation of your property is highly probable. There is quite a broad band of illegal exports, so if you are unsure about a prospective purchase, check that you are within the law. Examples of forbidden exports include national treasures of considerable importance, such as museum pieces and antique sculptures (with Italy in particular having lost several very important pieces over the years from illegal export). Forbidden items can also include animal products, such as products made from endangered species, including modern ivory or ancient bone sculptures, feathered items and snakeskin. Such items can, however, sometimes be imported or exported if they are sufficiently old, either antique or deemed to be of artistic importance, sometimes both.

Hunting for Buried Treasure

How often have you personally lost an article? It happens often, and all too easily. With a huge population, as in London, many items are lost every day. Even in Shakespeare's day the population was over 100,000, making it, even then, the largest city in Europe. Small wonder that things were concealed or buried when danger threatened, jettisoned into a convenient hole or river. Though often of little value, it is surprising how many objects still get picked up, and are then offered for resale in markets.

Many items still literally 'surface' in London, particularly in the wide channel of the River Thames. Tidal right up to Richmond, the Thames at low tide reveals a narrow central stream with long, flat stretches of mud and gravel to either side; when exposed, these banks can be a fertile ground for finding many ancient items. In fact, vast numbers of flint tools, swords and daggers have been found in the Thames, especially in the upper reaches of London. Clay pipes, too, are widely scattered in great numbers. Some of them probably date from the 17th century, at a time when smoking was supposed to ward off plague, and even children puffed – hence some rather small pipes.

But please note: there are specific laws regarding the ownership of valuable articles thus discovered. It is essential to declare your find – you may even be allowed to keep it. Furthermore, if it is officially examined and valued by experts, you will know exactly what type of buried treasure you have found.

Index

Page numbers in **bold** refer to illustrations in the text.